When JUST SAY NO Doesn't Work

What Everyone Needs to Know Now About the Changing Face of Today's Drug Use

by Joe Keil

Publisher: SynergEbooks, 11 Spruce Ct., Davenport, FL 33837

Printer: Fidlar Doubleday, 1515 East Kimberly Rd., Davenport, IA 52807

ISBN 978-0-7443-1571-4

Cover design: John Ernst Corporation, 1041 Rockledge Lane,
Neenah, WI 54956

Book design/back cover design: Patricia Rasch, pat_rasch@mac.com,
www.bookandcoverdesign.com

Author photo: Reische Photography

Select photographs: Wisconsin State Crime Lab, 4626 University Ave.,
Madison, WI 53705-2156

Editor: Sue Maves, 2106 Winnebago St., La Crosse, WI 54601

Drug Evaluation and Classification Training:
The Drug Recognition Expert School Instructor Manual/
Administrator Guide 2006.

Copyright holder: Joe Keil, May 2008

Author contact: Joe@whenjustsaynodoesntwork.com

Dedication

After starting this book several years ago I had given up because one famous individual discouraged me from authoring a book. While flying to Phoenix, Arizona to teach a class I had a very distinct feeling God was telling me to finish this book. I immediately reached for my computer and have been working on it ever since. As the book began to near completion God again stepped in and brought my wife to Bobbi Rodriguez at Fidlar Doubleday Books who agreed to take on this project. She then put us in contact with Deb Staples at SynergEbooks who took a chance on a new author and agreed to publish *When Just Say No Doesn't Work*. As our journey continued more people were introduced into our lives to make this book possible. John Ernst Corporation set up the book's web site, www.whenjustsaynodoesntwork.com. I thank you, Lord, for guiding me along and bringing so many people together from across the country to accomplish this task. It is you who provides me with the knowledge, abilities, and skills needed to provide this information to families who may be in crisis. You have watched over me while on duty always returning me safely home to my family at the end of my shift. With you anything is possible.

To my wife Deb, I don't even know where to begin to thank you for all you do for me and how I cherish our time together. You have stood by me and taken care of me on many days when my health was poor and my faith wavered. God has blessed you with a positive attitude and I hope you keep sharing it with those around you. Without you, this book would have stayed in my head, but thanks to your drive and commitment to this project, it has come to publication. I may have written it but you made it all possible. Much of your own work got put on hold to work on this book. A man can never out serve his wife she will always do more for him than he will ever do for her. I love you, Joe.

To my son, Zach, who since the age of eight years old has wanted to be a police officer, even though I told him to be a fireman, because no one hates firemen. You never wavered in your goal. You are such an eager student and your desire to learn is amazing. I am thankful for all your help in the R.U.S.H. classes we do together. I pray God watches over you throughout your career and you always return safely home. I'm very proud of the man you have become. Love you, dad.

For everyone afflicted with Adhesion Related Disorder (ARD), may we find peace and healing through the Lord.

Acknowledgements

My employment with the Manitowoc County Sheriff's Department was instrumental in my ability to attain the knowledge I have on drug use. It is a department that values continuing education and training, and I am grateful to them for the windows of opportunity they have provided. Carol Karstens was the Alcohol Program Manager for the Wisconsin Department of Transportation in 1995 and was instrumental in bringing the Drug Recognition Expert Program to the State of Wisconsin. As the program continued to grow, William Kraus retired from the City of Milwaukee Police Department and became Wisconsin State Drug Recognition Expert Coordinator. Due to his efforts and dedication to the DRE program, it has expanded to over one hundred Drug Recognition Experts in the State of Wisconsin.

I have instructed courses across the country and appreciate the quality of instructors and officers I have had the privilege to be associated with. Special thanks to Todd Cummings, Rob Kappelman, Jeff Meloy, Bill Kraus, Dave Catalano, Dan Feucht, Ron Lagosh, Dave Groves, Dan Delmore, Karen Schleis, Nate Thompson, John Gerschidmeyer, Stewart Ballweg, and a long list of others with whom I have spent countless hours sharing information and developing various programs. Many people I have met along the way tend to overlook officers from smaller agencies, but you cannot judge the officer on the size of his or her department, because many of them obtain a vast degree of knowledge in specialized areas.

Special thanks to the Wisconsin Crime Lab Ronald Groffy, and Robert Block for providing many of the close-up photographs of various drugs.

Table of Contents

Introduction

The United States has 5 percent of the world's population, yet consumes 60 percent of the world's illegal drugs—this does not include the abuse of legal drugs like Robitussin, Coricidin Cough and Cold, and a long list of others. The federal government estimates that 15 billion dollars of U.S. currency annually enters Mexico from the purchase of illegal drugs. Add to this the flow of cash going to other countries, such as Afghanistan, Pakistan, Burma, Laos, and Thailand, where several other types of controlled substances are illegally smuggled into the United States.

The drug trade is a multi-billion dollar industry. A kilo, or 1000 grams, of cocaine costs approximately $2000 in Columbia. Once it crosses the Texas/Mexico border, it now becomes worth about $10,000. As the drugs are transported north across the country, the value increases dramatically. In the Midwest that same kilo of cocaine has a street value of about $100 per gram, or $100,000, if uncut. When cut, the value can easily reach $300,000 to $400,000. The cutting of a drug simply means adding a similar substance to the drug to increase the amount. The purity will be less, but the quantity will multiply along with the profits.

Here are a few examples of drug use in the United States: New York City consumes approximately 10 tons of illegal drugs each day; Minneapolis/St. Paul consumes about 500 pounds of cocaine each month; the city of Baltimore has an estimated population of

600,000 people with approximately 10 percent of the population, or 60,000 people, addicted to heroin; in 2004, the law enforcement in the state of Missouri located 2,204 methamphetamine labs (how many were *not* located?); Wisconsin has a population of 5.5 million people with an estimated 1 million people abusing pharmaceutical drugs, that's about one-fifth of the population. Those are some startling statistics.

Many of us are unaware of the quantity of drugs that surround us within our own state, city, neighborhood, and local schools. The majority of Americans do not realize how this affects them and their families. Imagine a load of drugs headed toward this country from Mexico. If U.S. Customs, Homeland Security, and the Drug Enforcement Administration are unable to detect the drugs at the border, they continue to travel on our roadways into the heart of the country, heading toward *your* state. The drugs continue undetected past officers in bordering states and enter into your state getting past state police, deputy sheriffs, and local police officers. The drugs now enter into your county, city, or town still evading detection. They get into your schools, and now the drugs from as far away as Mexico are in the locker next to your child's. One day at school your child submits to peer pressure, and now the drugs are in your own home and poisoning your loved ones. It's too late now to believe drugs won't affect your family!

Still there are those who argue that drug use is a victimless crime, and that it should be legalized. Crimes are committed every minute across our country, which include burglaries, vehicle entries, thefts, homicides, sexual assaults, and a variety of crimes too long to list. Many of these crimes are committed for the purchase of drugs or the person committing the crime is under the influence of drugs at the time. In fact, 49 percent of Wisconsin inmates admit that they were under the influence of drugs when they committed their crime.

Drug use is rampant across the United States. Different areas of our country deal with different types of drugs, and the popularity of a drug increases and decreases as times change. Drug usage is nondiscriminatory; age, race, creed, color, nationality, sex, or economic status does not exclude anyone from falling victim to drug addiction.

There are three different levels of drug use: the first is recreational, the second is abuse, and the third is addiction. Recreational use is usually when drugs are taken with friends at a party or on an occasional weekend. The second level usually develops when the individual begins using drugs alone, not limiting the usage to just parties or weekends. The first and second levels are usually steps to the third level, where the user's life becomes consumed with the drug. At this point, jobs, families, and personal items are no longer regarded as important. I have talked with users who have sold the beds their children sleep in for cash to buy drugs. This is truly disheartening, as you can clearly see the family falling apart because of drug use.

Many parents are truly blind to the obvious. By this I mean our kids have a better understanding of drugs, what is available, how they work, and even the references made to them in various TV shows, movies, music recordings, and videos, than we imagine. As an example, in the movie *Scooby Doo 2: Monsters Unleashed,* there is a scene where Shaggy is seen spraying some whipped cream in Scooby Doo's mouth to make it look like Scooby Doo is foaming at the mouth. At the end of the scene, Shaggy holds the can upright and releases the propellant, which is nitrous oxide, and inhales it. This is a form of "huffing" and is a common way to ingest inhalants. Another example takes place on TV during a Simpson's episode. Homer is seen licking a toad. His pupils immediately dilate and he begins to hallucinate. The reference to the *Bufo alvarius* toad is the fact that it excretes bufotenine, a venom that when ingested produces an LSD-type high. TV shows and movies are replete with references to drug use. While we parents sit and watch these movies and programs with our children, we may not even be aware of the drug innuendos as we see our children laughing out loud at these drug-related references.

If you don't believe drugs can affect you or your family because of your social or economic status, look at recent court cases like Andrew Luster, one of the heirs to Max Factor cosmetics, who dosed unsuspecting females with GHB and then sexually assaulted them. Luster then fled to Mexico where he partied at bars and laid on the beach while warrants were issued for his arrest in California. United States' officials were having a difficult time extraditing Luster back to the United States because of Mexico's laws. Luster believed he was safe hiding out in Mexico until Dog the Bounty Hunter captured him, and Mexican officials were forced to turn Luster over to U.S. officials. In an ironic twist, Dog the Bounty Hunter and his assistants were arrested for bounty hunting, which is illegal in Mexico.

Other examples include Pete Rose Jr., who sold GBL to his minor league baseball teammates and was subsequently convicted and sentenced to one month in prison and five months of home detention. Brent Shapiro, the son of Robert Shapiro, one of the lawyers for O.J. Simpson, overdosed and died from a combination of ecstasy and alcohol. Anna Nichole Smith's son, Daniel, died from the mixture of several medications including antidepressants and methadone. A short time later Anna Nichole Smith, herself, died of a combination of antidepressant drugs. It is clear that having money and power does not exclude your family from the perils of drug use.

It is important to remember that knowledge is power. The

purpose of this book is to educate parents, teachers, and other professionals on the physical signs drugs produce on the human body, the terminology associated with different drugs, what drugs look like, and the paraphernalia associated with different categories of drugs. I hope this book gives you some insight into the drug-related dangers that your kids may be subjected to and that it becomes a valuable tool for your family.

Test Your Drug Knowledge

1. The term 420 refers to
   a. a random series of numbers.
   b. the use of LSD.
   c. marijuana use.
   d. has no meaning.

2. The nutmeg spice is being abused for its hallucinogenic effects.
   True or False?

3. Raves are safe dance parties where no alcohol or drugs are present.
   True or False?

4. Ecstasy elevates body temperature, and deaths have been recorded with temperatures of 110 degrees four hours after death.
   True or False?

5. Ketamine is
   a. an animal tranquilizer.
   b. is commonly referred to as Special K.
   c. is chemically related to PCP.
   d. All of the above.

6. Robitussin cough syrup is commonly consumed by kids for its intoxicating effects.
   True or False?

7. Morning Glory seeds are eaten or brewed in teas and consumed for hallucinogenic effects.
   True or False?

8. Which of the following terms refer to ecstasy use?
   a. XTC
   b. onE
   c. Adam
   d. All of the above

9. The white portion of a person's eyes will become markedly red from ingesting marijuana.
   True or False?

10. Prescription medications are obtained illegally
    a. by doctor shopping.
    b. burglary.
    c. during open houses when people are trying to sell their house.
    d. All of the above.

Answers to Questions:

Question 1: **C.** Marijuana. There are several different meanings. here are two of them: (1) It is the international time to smoke marijuana. (2) On April 20th of each year individuals should plant their marijuana seeds throughout the country, so as summer arrives marijuana will be growing everywhere.

Question 2: **True.** The common household spice can cause hallucinations when enough of the substance is ingested.

Question 3: **False.** At raves, drugs and alcohol are usually being abused by young adults.

Question 4: **True.** Ecstasy does elevate body temperature, usually to dangerous levels.

Question 5: **D.** All of the above.

Question 6: **True.** Robitussin or cough medicines that contain dextromethorphan are abused for the intoxicating effects.

Question 7: **True.** That's right. The seeds you buy at the store to plant in your flower garden are being abused for the hallucinogenic effects.

Question 8: **D.** All of the above refer to terms used for ecstasy.

Question 9: **True.** Marijuana is a vasodilator, which simply means it enlarges the blood vessels in the eyes.

Question 10: **D.** All of the above are methods used to obtain prescription medications.

CHAPTER 1

Drug Recognition
Expert Program

In the early 1970s the National Highway Traffic Safety Administration, in conjunction with the Los Angeles Police Department and the Southern California Research Institute developed the Drug Recognition Expert (DRE) Program. Two Los Angeles police officers, Len Leeds and Dick Studdard, along with Dr. Marcelline Burns, were instrumental in developing the Drug Recognition Expert Program. The course is designed to teach police officers how to recognize the signs and symptoms associated with drug use. The Drug Recognition Expert course is very intense with nine days of classroom instruction followed by a certification process where officers come in contact with individuals impaired by various substances and must be able to determine, based on their training, which drug category the individuals are under the influence of. The officers use a twelve-step process, which includes psychophysical tests, blood pressure, pulse rate, temperature, muscle tone, and observing a person's eyes in different lighting conditions. The officers' opinions regarding the impairment are confirmed by toxicology tests. This program was designed to aid officers in removing drug-impaired drivers from our nation's roadways. Even though the Drug Recognition Expert course has been in effect for over thirty years, not all states have these highly-trained officers available. This means that when a traffic stop or traffic crash occurs and the person was impaired by drugs, it may or may not be investigated to its fullest extent. The operator of the vehicle could simply walk away with only a minor citation.

In our society drunk driving is not always looked at as a crime unless the operator injured or killed someone. According to the National Highway Traffic Safety Administration, the average drunk driver commits the offense eighty times a year! The offenses for the average *drugged* driver are probably much greater than that. The following scenario is possible: your spouse, son, daughter, or loved one is traveling in a vehicle when a second vehicle fails to stop at a stop sign and strikes the vehicle being driven by your loved one. Serious injury or even death occurs. The operator of the other vehicle is unharmed and denies any use of alcohol. Many officers would simply determine whether the subject had been drinking alcohol and have them submit to a portable breath test. If no alcohol was noted, the subject would either receive a citation for failure to stop at a stop sign or be charged with homicide by negligence or reckless driving of a motor vehicle. Keep in mind that this will depend on the laws of the state in which you reside and how the district attorney determines whether a citation or a criminal charge is applicable. Now consider that the operator of the second vehicle was smoking marijuana four hours prior to the crash. Could the use of marijuana from several hours earlier still be affecting him? The answer is yes!

The officer may not even recognize the physical signs of impairment caused by the earlier marijuana use and fail to investigate the incident properly. A Drug Recognition Expert officer would likely be able to determine the category or categories of drugs a person ingested and whether that person was impaired at the time of the crash. This can easily mean the difference between justice and injustice. The suspect is not the only one with rights. What about the victim and the victim's family and their rights? If this infuriates you the way it does me, determine if your state has a Drug Recognition Expert Program. If not, call your legislator and raise awareness for the program.

Several other programs have been developed because of the Drug Recognition Expert Program. The one that most pertains to the subject of this book is the Drug Impairment Training for Educational Professionals (DITEP). This program is designed to assist teachers, social workers, probation and parole agents, and health care professionals to detect signs of drug use.

This book contains much of the DITEP information which is equally beneficial to parents. It also goes into great detail regarding the paraphernalia associated with drugs, street terms associated with each of the seven drug categories, and some of the household items that individuals have discovered new uses for.

As mentioned, there are seven major drug categories. Each category produces different effects on the human body. Each drug in a particular category can produce similar effects as the other drugs in that category. One example would be that of alcohol. Alcohol is a central nervous system depressant. The use of alcohol can produce thick, slurred speech; drowsiness; droopy eyes; uncoordinated sluggish reactions; and an odor of intoxicants, along with other effects. Other drugs within the depressant category, like Xanax, Prozac, Zoloft, and Valium, can produce the same effects as alcohol without the odor of alcohol.

Each of the upcoming chapters will be broken down to identify specific categories of drugs and explain the physical effects, time and duration of the effects, the drug paraphernalia specific to each

category, and the street terms associated with each category.
The seven drug categories are as follows:

(1) central nervous system depressants,
(2) central nervous system stimulants,
(3) hallucinogens,
(4) dissociative anesthetics,
(5) narcotic analgesics,
(6) inhalants,
(7) marijuana.

CHAPTER 2

Drug Categories in Relation to the Eyes

In order to understand future chapters, it is necessary to understand the effects drugs have on the eyes. It's said a person's eyes are "the windows to the soul." The eyes tell the story about what a person is doing or has been doing. Our eyes work together as a team, and drugs affect that team in a predictable fashion.

All the drug categories will affect the eyes in some way. Certain drugs will cause the pupils to dilate, others will cause pupils to constrict, and still others will not affect the pupil size but will produce Horizontal Gaze Nystagmus (HGN), which is an involuntary jerking of the eyes. Law enforcement officers are instructed during specific classes on how to determine HGN, so it is not something we can effectively cover in a handbook. What we will deal with in this book is the effect drugs have on the pupil size.

Using the old standard regarding the average size of a person's pupils, which is between 3.0 and 6.5 mm, is much easier to understand than the new standard, which uses different lighting conditions in relationship to the pupil size. If a person goes outside on a very bright and sunny day, the pupils constrict to around 3.0 to 4.0 mm in size. Now let's say it is nighttime and if we go outside in the dark, our pupils dilate to around 6.5 mm in size. The reaction to the change in light is immediately observable in the pupil. The body does not have to think about reacting to the change; it is autonomic.

When certain drugs are introduced into the body, the pupils' size can become dilated (larger) or constricted (smaller). The reaction to light can also be slowed down to where you can actually see the pupil slowly changing in size. There can also be little or no reaction to light, because the pupils are constricted as far as they can go.

PUPILLOMETER
MILLIMETERS

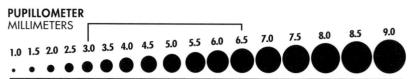

The chart above shows the average sizes of pupils. However, there are always exceptions to the rule, and some individuals will be outside the norm without the use of drugs. Other factors can cause pupil dilation, such as fear, certain eye drops, diabetic shock, and many other causes. If you notice unequal pupil sizes, in which one pupil is dilated and the other pupil is constricted, this condition is medical and not caused by drug use. Several factors can cause unequal pupils, including an old or recent head injury, a glass eye, a tumor, or even just a natural condition. The eyes work as a team, and when drugs are ingested, both eyes are affected in the same manner.

Now let's look at the eye; the iris is the colored portion of the eyeball with the pupil contained within the iris. We know the lack of light will cause the pupil to get bigger and that bright light will cause the constriction of the pupil. The pupil is considered dilated if it is covering more than one-half of the iris. Remember, the eyes act as a team. Now let's try an experiment: shine a light in someone's right eye and watch the left eye. It also constricts. This demonstrates how the eyes act as a team. When drugs are ingested into the body, both eyes are affected.

If a person's pupils are dilated, it indicates one of three categories of drugs: hallucinogens, stimulants, or marijuana. This means any drug within those categories may dilate the eyes. For example, the hallucinogen category contains some of the following drugs: peyote, psilocybin mushrooms, LSD and a host of others, and all may dilate the eyes. The same is true for stimulants and marijuana. There are also a few exceptions in the depressant category which may dilate the eyes such as Soma, Quaaludes, methaqualone and products containing dextromethorphan. However, we must also keep in mind that if a person has generally small pupils and they ingest one of the drugs that dilate the pupil, it is possible for the person to still be within the larger side of normal. We also have to realize that because each human being has chemical differences, at times the pupils may not always dilate when consuming hallucinogens, stimulants, or marijuana.

Narcotic analgesics are the only category of drugs that will constrict the pupils. When ingesting any drug from this category, like heroin, OxyContin, and a long list of others, the pupils of the eyes will constrict and may be about the size of a pinhead.

Next let's look at the white portion of the eye; some drugs will cause vasoconstriction, while others will cause vasodilatation. Vasoconstriction is the constricting of blood vessels within the white portion of the eye, while vasodilatation is the expansion of those blood vessels. Cocaine is a vasoconstrictor and in liquid form can be used in eye, nose, and throat surgery as it can rapidly stop bleeding. If a small amount of liquid cocaine is placed into the eye, it will cause the blood vessels to constrict and the eye will be extremely white. Marijuana, alcohol, and products containing dextromethorphan will cause the white portion of the eye to become markedly red. In other words, it dilates the blood vessels within the white portion of the eye. Many drug users are aware of the redness caused by ingesting the drugs and carry bottles of Visine with them.

Lastly, there is Ptosis, which is simply droopy eyes, and generally occurs with depressants and narcotics as individuals can become very sleepy from the drugs.

I can't begin to tell you the number of traffic stops I have made that completely changed from routine stops to a drug trafficking stop by simply looking into the subject's eyes. The first thing I do when talking with anyone is to look directly into their eyes to determine if their pupils are of equal size, if they are dilated, constricted, or within the normal range, and also if the eyes are bloodshot and glassy. This is only the first clue of possible drug use. There are also behavioral and physical signs that indicate drug usage as well. Unlike medical conditions that generally affect a particular area or even one side of the body, i.e., stroke, drugs affect the entire body.

How do drugs affect all systems of the body? The following is an example of how multiple systems of the body can be affected by drug use. A person ingests a narcotic such as heroin via hypodermic needle. The skin is affected at the injection site, and repeated injections cause ulcerations and abscesses to form leading to the collapse of veins. Narcotics can also cause histamines to be released into the body, which causes itching. The heroin also creates a euphoric feeling, which can include drowsiness, depressed reflexes, nausea, and a long list of other physical effects. It also dries out the vocal cords causing a low raspy voice and even affects the bodily function of eliminating waste. The colon becomes dry and it is difficult to eliminate stool. This is the beginning of understanding the physiology of drugs and their effects on the body.

CHAPTER 3

Physiology of Drugs

First of all, don't be afraid to read this chapter. It may sound complicated, but it is going to be very basic and will provide insight as to why things happen to our body when drugs are ingested. Drugs enter the body in a variety of ways and must get to the brain in order to impair a person. If our head were removed from our body and drugs entered the body, there would be no effect. This would be impossible, but it does show that all drugs, when ingested, attach themselves to receptor sites in the brain and basically fool the brain into releasing chemicals, which cause a variety of responses. Drugs affect the body in a predictable fashion, as we will see in future chapters. Because drug abuse causes the body to develop a tolerance to a drug, users need to ingest larger and larger quantities to obtain the same intoxicating effect.

Drugs affect all systems of the body, including both sides of the body. Medical conditions generally affect one system of the body or possibly only one side of the body. A stroke victim usually loses control of one side of the body, because the medical condition affected that one side. Substance abuse will affect both sides of the body and all of the body's systems.

There are eleven major systems of the human body, and each one of these systems can be affected by ingesting various drugs.

The eleven systems of the body are the muscular, urinary, reproductive, digestive, endocrine, respiratory, skeletal, integumentary, nervous, immune, and circulatory systems. How is each system affected? Let's break down each one and give an example of how each system is affected. First, the muscular system—depressants and narcotics cause muscle tone to become very flaccid, while stimulants and dissociative anesthetics cause muscle rigidity.

The urinary system is affected by drugs like alcohol or ecstasy, which cause frequent urination and dehydrates a person. The reproductive system is affected because drugs like ecstasy can cause erectile dysfunction, and the opposite is true of amyl nitrites, which cause erections. The digestive system is affected by drugs that are stimulants. Stimulants are appetite suppressants, thus most diet pills contain some type of stimulant. The opposite is true of marijuana use, which increases appetite. The endocrine system is in charge of the release of hormones, which generally are not affected by the use of street drugs. Hormonal problems are usually controlled by prescription medications. The respiratory system is usually affected by drugs that are smoked attributing to asthma, emphysema, lung cancer, and a host of other pulmonary disorders. The skeletal system can be affected by a weakened immune system causing a break down in bone density, which generally happens over extended periods of drug use. The integumentary system is otherwise known as the skin, hair, finger and toe nails; and its primary function is to provide protection to the rest of the systems of the body. It is affected in several ways as drugs like stimulants and narcotics, when ingested, can cause histamines to be released into our bodies causing the user to itch or pick at their skin. If a person injects drugs into their veins, skin, or arteries ulcerations and infections can occur.

Many of the drugs being injected were not intended to be

injected, but users are creative in their methods of ingestion. Drugs themselves are caustic, and the body is immediately trying to eliminate them from the system. In fact, many of the drugs are cut or adulterated with other chemicals and those chemicals, are also being introduced into the body. Finally, the fact that many users share or use dirty needles also leads to skin infections or the transfer of AIDS, HIV, hepatitis, and other various diseases.

Within the nervous system there are two categories of nerves, the afferent and efferent nerves. The afferent, or sensory, nerves send messages from the body to the brain; e.g., when we touch something hot, our body sends a message to our brain telling the brain the item is hot. The efferent, or motor, nerves carry messages from the brain to the body. The efferent nerves contain two sub-categories: the voluntary nerves control the movements of our arms, legs, etc., and the autonomic nerves control the heart rate, blood pressure, pupil dilation, etc. There are two different types of autonomic nerves: the sympathetic and the parasympathetic nerves. Sympathetic nerves control fight or flight response and speed up the body, while the parasympathetic nerves slow the body down. When drugs are ingested, each one of these systems is affected by either slowing down or speeding up the body. For example, if a person ingested cocaine, which is a stimulant, it basically fools the body into speeding up, elevating blood pressure, pulse, and body temperature. Finally, the circulatory system can be sped up by ingesting stimulants or slowed down by taking narcotics. These are only a few examples, and as we talk about each category, we will have a better understanding of each drug's affect on the body.

The common methods of ingesting drugs are smoking, snorting, injecting, orally, inhaling, rectally, and by transdermal absorption. This leads us to the question of which is the fastest way drugs affect our body. Most people believe it is injecting, however, smoking or inhaling is the fastest way for drugs to affect our brain. Smoking or inhaling is usually only faster by a few seconds and is less if the person injecting utilizes the artery in the neck. Most users inject into a vein that carries deoxygenated blood, which travels to the heart, then to the lungs to become oxygenated, and then back to the heart, and on to the brain. When smoking or inhaling drugs, the chemical goes directly to the lungs where oxygenated blood travels directly to the brain via the heart. Once in the brain the drug fools the brain into releasing chemicals like dopamine, serotonin, and a host of others. The type of drug ingested will relate to the type of chemicals the brain chooses to release. The method of ingestion can, however, affect the portion of the body by which it was administered. An example of this would be if one person injects heroin and another snorts heroin. The physical effects on the body would be the same but the duration of the effect could change: in addition, the area of the body where the injection took place could become ulcerated and infected. The effect on the nose from snorting the heroin could cause ulceration or bleeding. Over time the heroin could also cause a deterioration of the septum, creating an opening between the nostrils. Smoking various drugs also causes severe damage to the lungs, leading to chronic bronchitis, emphysema, and tumors.

Some users will place a liquid form of a drug into an eye dropper and place the drops into the eyes. This is generally ineffective as the drug would have to go through the tear duct which runs into the sinuses. Most often the liquid in the eye drop container is placed under the tongue or in open cuts. As you can see, the method of ingestion severely affects a particular portion of the body; but as we read each chapter, we will see that no matter what the method of ingestion is each particular category of drugs will affect the body in their own predictable fashion.

One of the interesting arguments by advocates for drug use is that—since our brain contains receptor cites for heroin, marijuana, and a host of other drugs, our body must have been created to use these drugs, otherwise the receptor cites would not have been created. The reason that argument doesn't make sense is because our body also uses chemical messengers that utilize some of the same receptor sites that drugs attach themselves to, to control mood, thought, and various senses.

Lastly, there is homeostasis, a kind of regulator for our bodies. Homeostasis is basically a balance of salts, waters, and sugars. When a person ingests drugs, our natural balance is disrupted. Our regulator generally keeps our body temperature around 98.6° Fahrenheit, our pulse usually around 60 to 90 beats per minute, and our blood pressure at 120 to 140 for systolic and 70 to 90 for diastolic. Again, these are averages and can vary depending on age, weight, and medical issues. When a drug is ingested, like cocaine, the body's reaction causes an increase in body temperature, and elevates the pulse and blood pressure. The cocaine basically fools the brain to warm the body and in turn, increase the pulse and blood pressure. Homeostasis is disrupted and the body begins to release chemicals to cool it down, and to lower the pulse and blood pressure.

One of my personal favorite actors, John Belushi, died of a speedball, which is a mixture of cocaine and heroin. The cocaine elevates the body temperature, pulse rate, blood pressure, and a host of other physical signs. The brain immediately releases chemicals to bring the body back down to normal ranges, and at roughly the same time the cocaine wears off the narcotic began to exhibit its effects. The narcotic lowers body temperature, pulse, blood pressure, respiration, and a host of other effects. Another speedball is consumed by Belushi and the cocaine again elevates the body's systems. The body is now unsure what chemicals to release—should it release chemicals to speed up or slow down in order to bring the body back to homeostasis. In the end, the narcotic slows the pulse rate, blood pressure, and respiration to a point where a person goes unconscious and dies. This sounds like a fairly easy way to pass away, which is farthest from the truth. Overdosing is a very painful way to die.

CHAPTER 4

Other Resources

As your children age, you continue to see behavior, health, and physical changes associated with development. The majority of changes observed are those regarding growth; consequently, you should not overlook resources such as the family doctor or dentist. The family doctor or dentist routinely maintains a chart on your child from when they were first born until their current age and has a general understanding of their health. As you take your child to doctors and dentists for their yearly checkups, you should be asking questions about what they find. You should also be discussing any behavioral, emotional, and physical changes you are noticing. A doctor may not see the physiological effects drugs have on your child if the drugs were not used recently; however, this is where your observations can be key, as some drugs when ingested can permanently affect your child's behaviors and moods. Discuss your concerns with the doctor and if applicable request a drug test be conducted, but bear in mind toxicology tests are limited and cannot always detect drug use. Ask the doctor which drugs the lab can test for? Not all drugs are detectable from a blood test. What level does the lab test down to? Drug tests measure the amount of drugs in the human body in nanograms, and very few labs test to zero nanograms because of cost issues. What I mean by this is, if a person smokes marijuana and the level of the drug used is 45 nanograms and if the lab only tests to a level of 50 nanograms, the blood test would come back negative even though the marijuana was consumed.

Medical professionals do not always understand the physical signs and symptoms of street drug use or the effects large doses of over-the-counter medications have on the body. When doctors prescribe medications, it is their belief the patient will follow the recommended dosages and times. They are under the assumption the drug will not be consumed for recreational purposes. You cannot rely totally on a doctor to recognize if your child may be involved in drug use; however, it is an opportunity to obtain a professional opinion and may help in detecting drug use.

The following is an actual scenario of one doctor's limited knowledge regarding the abuse of over-the-counter medications. A DRE officer arrives at a residence in Germantown, Wisconsin. He recognizes that the teenager has overdosed on Robitussin and calls for medical assistance. The child is rushed to the hospital via ambulance. While at the hospital, the officer tells the emergency room doctor that the teenager overdosed on dextromethorphan. The doctor's response was, "What's that?" The officer informed him it is used in Robitussin and that the teenager drank several bottles of it. The doctor's response was, "Why would he do that?" Again, knowledge is power and educating ourselves and others can be instrumental in possibly saving your child's life.

A dentist is also another asset as certain drugs will cause specific signs in the oral cavity, such as a green or brown coating on the tongue or teeth. Dentists can also detect the unusual loss of the enamel coating protecting the teeth or possibly that the teeth have been ground down or broken off from constant grinding. They will also observe the gum line and determine if it has become soft, ulcerated, or inflamed. Again, each one of these conditions is specific to drug use and will be discussed later.

As I stated earlier, the medical professionals' knowledge about street drugs and their use is limited to their experience with drug users. If a doctor has never observed an individual under the influence of Robitussin cough syrup, cocaine, heroin, or a variety of other drugs, it will be difficult for him to determine what is causing the problem. The emergency room doctor will treat the symptoms of the problem but not necessarily determine the cause of the problem.

Here is a true story of two parents from an upper middle class family who were seeking help for their daughter's health issues. The mother is a friend of mine, who was present at a class where I was instructing a course on drug recognition. She began to ask questions regarding heroin use. The questions were far beyond what I considered normal, and during a break I asked her why she had such an interest in a particular drug. At this point she informed me her now twenty-one-year-old daughter had been a heroin addict since she was nineteen and had experimented with marijuana, mushrooms and ecstasy since age sixteen. As I spoke with her she informed me her family was completely taken off guard when their daughter's boyfriend called and informed them of their daughter's drug use. She stated her daughter was in the high school band and was carrying a GPA in which she would graduate with honors.

Since graduating high school, her daughter's life has taken a turn for the worse; she was sick for the past two years and had been to numerous doctors who could not determine what was wrong. During that time no one ordered a toxicological test for drugs. Finally, the mom requested the doctors conduct a blood test on the daughter, which came back positive for opiates. Her daughter then admitted to heroin use. Again, keep in mind that there are thousands of drugs that go undetected in toxicological screens, which will be discussed later. It was only after the daughter admitted she had been using heroin that her mom understood the signs that seemed strange at the time but were overlooked because she never thought her daughter would be involved with drug use. She has since found help and recovered from her addictions.

Examples she shared with me of the indicators of drug use, which were never questioned at the time, were wearing sweaters and long sleeve shirts during the summer to hide track marks and sunglasses at night to hide the constricted pupils. She also located cotton balls about the size of a pea and bottle caps in her daughter's bedroom. These items are consistent with the use of illegal drugs. These are only a few examples of behaviors that we can disregard as meaningless until we learn what behaviors are consistent with drug abuse and items used in the drug world. Again, as we delve into each chapter, I will explain the use of the paraphernalia associated with each drug.

It is not my intention to make everyone paranoid that their child is using drugs. However, I want you to keep an open mind and not overlook obvious behaviors by simply thinking "not my child" or "my child wouldn't use drugs." Sometimes it is difficult to determine drug use from the normal changes a teenager goes through—the moodiness, withdrawn attitude, less dependence on family, and a host of other emotional and physical changes—but please remember, drugs are nondiscriminatory and can affect anyone. When we try to determine drug use, we don't just look at one behavior. It is an accumulation of multiple behaviors, indicators, and the knowledge we will gain as we continue to read.

Another great resource to find out what drugs are being abused in your area is to take the time to make an appointment and speak with a police school resource officer. These officers generally have a better rapport with young adults than that of a patrol officer. Kids give the resource officers so much information about what is going on in the school and community regarding gangs, drugs, parties, and much more. The kids provide the resource officers with information they would never tell a uniformed police officer or a parent. If you really want insight as to what your child's behaviors are at school, speak with the resource officer.

The Scheduling of Drugs

The Drug Enforcement Administration (DEA) is the federal law enforcement agency in control of scheduling drugs. The scheduling basically puts the drug into a category of being illegal drugs or legal drugs that require a prescription. Drugs are scheduled in classes I through V. A schedule I drug is illegal, highly addictive, and has no medical use within the United States. A schedule II drug is less addictive than a schedule I drug and has some medical use within the United States but is highly regulated. Schedules III through V are gradually less addictive, less restrictive, and all have medical use within the United States and require a prescription.

CHAPTER 5

Depressants

Depressants are drugs that cause a general state of relaxation, drowsiness, sluggish reactions, and disorientation. Alcohol is the number one abused drug that falls into the depressant category. You may be surprised to learn what other common items contain alcohol and are being abused.

Anyone under the age of twenty-one cannot legally go into a store to purchase beer or hard liquor, which range from 4 to 90 percent alcohol, yet a child of any age can go to a grocery store and purchase pure peppermint extract which is 89 percent alcohol or 178 proof. Wow! Many of our household food flavorings like imitation rum extract, almond extract, and many others contain alcohol. Drinking pure peppermint extract or any of the food flavorings containing alcohol may be difficult to consume straight from the bottle; however, the flavorings can be mixed with a variety of sodas or other liquids for easier consumption. This disguises the alcohol, and the person can discretely become intoxicated while at high school dances or in front of parents or peers.

Many mouthwash products also contain ethanol, which is the alcohol intended for human consumption. For this reason many teenagers purchase these products to achieve the same intoxicating results one can achieve from consuming alcohol. Again, simply being aware of numerous empty bottles of mouthwash or flavor extracts may help you in detecting behaviors you previously never observed.

There are many new products on the market today that contain both alcohol and a stimulant (caffeine). Here are a few examples: Sparks, Mezzanine, DNA and Nitro. Several also contain guarana, taurine, ginseng, milk thistle and fruit flavors; many of these ingredients also act as stimulants when consumed. "Ice Shots," which is frozen alcohol on a stick or in a cup, can be purchased over the internet. This product is a mixture of alcohol and fruit juices and contains 10–20 percent alcohol. Parents easily mistake these products as a frozen fruit bar.

Understanding Alcohol

There are three different types of alcohol: ethanol, isopropanol, and methanol. Ethanol is the alcohol intended for human consumption and is contained in many products *(photo 5.1)*. As we drink alcohol, it travels into the stomach. Several factors are now affecting how fast the alcohol will be absorbed into our bodies. If we just consumed a large meal, it is difficult to become intoxicated; because the pylorus valve which allows food or drinks to pass into the small intestine is closed. Digestive enzymes are now being released and begin to break down the food and alcohol. How fast we eliminate alcohol depends on whether we have a fast or slow metabolism. If we consume alcohol on an empty stomach, the pylorus valve remains open and alcohol flows into the small intestine and into the bloodstream, where it travels to the brain and impairs our thoughts, coordination, balance, and a long list of other effects.

The percent of alcohol is one-half of what the "proof" is. Example: a bottle of Jack Daniels is 45 percent alcohol or 90 proof. It does not matter the type of alcoholic drink ingested, as each one will contain approximately the same amount of pure ethanol. A 12-ounce can of beer contains 0.48 ounces of pure ethanol, a 4-ounce glass of wine contains 0.48 ounces of pure ethanol, and a 1 ¼-ounce shot of 80 proof whiskey contains 0.50 ounces of pure ethanol. If an average 175 pound male consumes one drink, his blood alcohol content (BAC) would be approximately 0.018. Therefore, it does not matter the type of alcoholic beverage consumed—the blood alcohol content would be approximately the same.

If a female weighing the same consumed the same drink as a male, her blood alcohol content would be higher. This is because males have more water in their bodies while females have more fatty tissue, which is designed to protect the unborn child in the womb. In fact, it only takes one-half of the drink for the female to obtain a BAC of 0.015.

Male bodies are comprised of approximately 68 percent water, while female bodies are approximately 55 percent water. Since alcohol is attracted to water, and male bodies have more water, there are more areas for the alcohol to disperse to. Alcohol is attracted to areas of the body that contain a lot of water like the brain, liver, and muscle tissue. Alcohol is not attracted to bones or fatty tissue.

Some alcohol is eliminated from the body by sweat, tears, breath, and urine; however, the majority of alcohol is eliminated from the body by the liver. That is why alcoholics develop cirrhosis of the liver. Through a chemical process, the alcohol is burned in the liver at a rate of approximately 0.015 percent per hour depending on a person's metabolism.

Let's do some math. If an average 175 pound man consumes ten beers in an hour, his blood alcohol would be approximately 0.15–0.18. This can vary if the person had a very large meal or has a fast or slow metabolism. If alcohol is eliminated from the body at a rate of approximately 0.015 percent per hour, it would take about ten hours to return to a BAC of 0.00. This is why it is virtually impossible for a person to be arrested for drunk driving from having a before and after dinner drink. By the time your meal arrives and you eat, the first drink is already eliminated from the body. The one after-dinner drink will not cause a person to obtain a BAC of 0.08, which is the standard for drunken driving arrests in most states.

You may have heard of the old remedy of giving an intoxicated or drunk person coffee or some type of stimulant to sober them up. The only thing you're going to end up with is a wide awake drunk! The only way for a person to eliminate the majority of alcohol from their system is time.

Alcohol is generally ingested by drinking; however, several other methods for consuming alcohol do exist including injection, vaporizing and then inhaling the alcohol, and even by enema. As strange as some of these methods of ingestion sound, there are reasons for them. By vaporizing the alcohol, it travels directly into the lungs that carry oxygenated blood to the brain. Products on the market include the Volcano Vaporizer and AWOL, meaning alcohol without liquid. The AWOL product mixes distilled spirits with pure oxygen where it can then be inhaled or snorted, again, traveling directly into the bloodstream.

Via enema is another method of ingestion because the stomach is being bypassed and alcohol goes directly into the colon, into the bloodstream, and to the brain. With both of these methods of ingestion, the odor of alcohol will still be present on a person's breath, because alcohol travels throughout the bloodstream and the breath is an area where it is also eliminated.

Over-the-Counter Medications

Next are the over-the-counter medications. Drugs that fall into this category are products such as Robitussin, Coricidin Cough and Cold (CCC), NyQuil, Delsym or any products containing dextromethorphan, also known as DXM *(photo 5.2)*. The effects of the products containing dextromethorphan can vary depending on the amount ingested. In the normal recommended dosage Robitussin, CCC, and Delsym give relief of coughing, sinus pressure, and flu symptoms. Taking moderate doses above the recommended amount can cause symptoms of intoxication. A person can have difficulty walking, appear drowsy, and have slurred speech with a general drunk-like appearance. If a person consumes large amounts of dextromethorphan, the effects can mimic that of dissociative anesthetics and can last for up to twelve hours. The higher doses generally consist of consuming 8–10 bottles of Robitussin or a 24-pack of CCC. If a person is conscious, they may exhibit nausea and can have a blank stare, cyclic mood swings, hallucinations, inability to feel pain, and possibly become violent. A person can also be unresponsive and difficult to awaken, and you may believe that they are in a coma. Even though most depressants lower pulse rates, the products containing dextromethorphan elevate pulse rates and also dilate the pupils. As with most depressants, the white portion of a person's eyes will become markedly red.

Again, the active ingredient in these over-the-counter medications that causes the impairment is dextromethorphan. Kids involved in the abuse of this drug know that drinking several bottles of Robitussin will cause you to vomit, so many have switched to the blister packs of Coricidin Cough and Cold HBP (high blood pressure). This switch produces the same effects as Robitussin but without causing the user to vomit. Kids also know that Coricidin

Cough and Cold HBP contain the highest levels of DXM available on the market (30 mg).

Ingesting CCC is commonly referred to as "skittling" like the candy Skittles, because CCC tablets are often taken out of their blister packs and put in with Skittles to disguise their appearance. They can then be consumed anywhere in the presence of anyone and believed to be candy. Another way to ingest CCC is by drilling a hole through the center of the CCC tablets and then placing them on candy necklaces to again disguise the tablets. A general term for ingesting multiple CCC tablets is called "flat packing," which typically indicates ingesting the entire blister pack of pills at one time.

Kids know that Delsym cough syrup also contains the highest amount of DXM (30 mg) available in over-the-counter cough medicine, which also contains 26 percent alcohol. Delsym cough syrup, because of its orange color and taste, is often mixed with orange soda to give the appearance of ingesting a common drink. Delsym also offers an alcohol-free cough syrup.

Kids have also learned how to extract the DXM from the products. It is as easy as pouring the liquid cough syrup through a coffee filter. As the liquid dries, the DXM is extracted and remains on top of the coffee filter where it can then be smoked or snorted. Another method to extract dextromethorphan is to mix equal amounts of Robitussin cough syrup with ammonia; as the two products mix, a separation takes place. The lower fluid becomes clear and the top layer is colored. The clear fluid is drained into a container and then heated with a blow dryer until a white powder forms. The white powder is pure dextromethorphan and can then be snorted, smoked, or injected.

Users also combine drug categories. A common combination is called "Robo fire," which is ingesting large amounts of Robitussin followed by inhaling lighter fluid which has been soaked or saturated in a rag. The effects of the two drugs are overwhelming and can also be deadly.

Benadryl is an over-the-counter drug being abused in both liquid and tablet form. Benadryl is commonly used for hives, rashes, and to relieve allergy symptoms. The active ingredient that causes impairment is diphenhydramine. In low doses it mimics the effects of alcohol; in larger doses it can cause hallucinations.

The same can be said for the motion sickness pills, Dramamine. In lower doses it causes similar effects as alcohol, but in higher doses it can cause hallucinations. The active ingredient in the Dramamine causing the impairment is dimenhydrinate, a chemical cousin to diphenhydramine. Recently I observed an eighteen-year-old male who ingested twenty-five Dramamine tablets and was hallucinating vividly and talking with a little green man who was floating on the ceiling at the hospital. When asked why he had taken so much of the drug, he stated he was with some friends and was experimenting to see what would happen.

You're probably wondering what a high dose is. Remember, I stated drugs are body weight-dose equivalent. This simply means we can't give a specific amount as it is dependant on the weight of the user and whether a tolerance to the drug has occurred. Another factor is the type and purity of a drug along with the possibility of multiple drug categories being ingested. Generally, following the recommended dose on the manufacture's label does not cause impairment.

⚑ Red Flags for Parents

Red flags for parents are common terms like "going Robo, Tussin, CCC or Triple C, DXM, Red Devils, Skittling, Sylum, Orange Drink, and O.J. I can't stress enough the need to pay attention to your child's clothing, covers to books, folders, and any scribbling regarding these terms. As alcohol is always a concern, you may want to mark liquor bottles to see if any has been removed or if it has been watered down. Remember to also look for numerous mouthwash or food extract bottles as their ingredients may contain alcohol. You may also want to keep track of other alcohol you have in the house.

Prescription Medications

Prescription drugs are being sold and abused by kids and adults across the country; however, it is impossible to write about every prescribed medication that falls within the depressant category. The depressant category contains subcategories that include antipsychotic, antianxiety tranquilizers, antidepressants, barbiturates, nonbarbiturates, and combinations with multiple drugs mixed together.

Many drugs are prescribed to help a person cope with difficult emotional problems, chemical imbalances, sleep disorders, and the stress of physical health problems. Prescription medications within the depressant category affect the body much like alcohol, but can be more potent or less potent depending on the type and amount ingested. As mentioned earlier, drugs can be body weight-dose equivalent, meaning if a person takes the prescribed amount of a drug, it may or may not cause impairment. It is like drinking a half a can of beer. Depending on how often you drink, how much you weigh, and your sex, you will probably not feel any effects from drinking only a half a can of beer.

The same is true of medication to a certain degree, because the amount of drug dosages vary for each person. The type of drug ingested also causes variations on what the effects will be. Some prescribed medications will cause physical impairment with one dose, while others will not. Durations of the effects vary by the substance ingested, the method in which it was ingested, and the amount taken.

Depressants are ingested for the sedative and euphoric effects they create and are also used in combination with alcohol to enhance intoxification. They are also ingested by stimulant and narcotic users to soften withdrawal symptoms and are often referred to as "landing gear."

There are thousands of prescription medications available. The following is a list of some of the most commonly abused depressants: alprazolam (Xanax) *(photo 5.3)*, fluoxetine (Prozac), (Librium) chlordiazepoxide, carisoprodol (Soma), zaleplon, (Sonata), lorazepam (Ativan), and zolpidem (Ambien) *(photo 5.4, 5.5)*, clonazepam (Klonopin) *(photo 5.6)*, (Seroquel) quetiapine fumarate, diazepam (Valium) *(photo 5.7)*.

Soma is used to treat muscle strains and spasms and users often take it in combination with alcohol to enhance the effects. Soma is also very addictive.

Ambien and Sonata are sleep aids and are used to treat insomnia. Users enjoy the hallucination they experience while trying to stay awake fighting the drugs' effects.

Clonazepam (Klonopin) is an anticonvulsant and is used in the treatment of seizures and is also an antianxiety medication. Cocaine, heroin and OxyContin users are also abusing Klonopin to help in treating anxiety, especially when the effects of the drugs they ingested wear off.

One of the top abused pharmacological drugs is lorazepam; it is used as a tranquilizer to treat mild to severe anxiety, tension, and depression. It is very often used in combination with alcohol. Cocaine users also use this drug to ease the effects produced when the cocaine is wearing off.

Seroquel is an antipsychotic medication and is commonly abused.

Xanax is available in pill form and also in a 2 milligram tablet, which is commonly referred to among teens as "zaney bars."

Again, the ingestion of the recommended dose of a prescription medication is unlikely to cause impairment; it is when drugs are ingested at abuse levels or are used in combinations that individuals become impaired.

As we continue to understand each category of drugs, we will also see the variation in the effects from the drug categories and even the exception within each category. As with almost any drug, an overdose can result in coma or death if the prescribed amount is abused.

Obtaining Prescription Medications

The ingestion of prescription pills among teenagers is increasing at an alarming rate. So, how do kids or adults obtain prescription medications? The first method is called "doctor shopping," which is going to multiple doctors and obtaining the preferred medications the individual desires. Kids and adults will fake injuries, migraine headaches, gastrointestinal problems, or depression to obtain desired prescriptions. Red flags would be prescriptions that are continually lost or stolen, asking for specific drugs by name, or claims that certain drugs are not effective and request a more potent form.

Occasionally prescription pads are stolen from medical offices and users forge the doctor's name to obtain fraudulent prescriptions. Prescriptions are then filled and the pills are abused or can also be sold at inflated prices. These methods are generally used more by adults than kids, especially if parents are the providers of the insurance, because insurance statements will indicate the numerous doctor visits.

One clever method to obtaining prescription medications is

going to real estate open houses. When walking through homes for sale, individuals will use the bathroom and then search the medicine cabinet and remove prescriptions. By the time the homeowner realizes the medications are missing the perpetrator is long gone. Even if law enforcement was called immediately and the open house attracted a large volume of people, it is nearly impossible to determine who removed the prescriptions. These again are generally adult crimes.

The easiest way for kids to attain medications is by simply looking in the medicine cabinet, whether it is at home, a grandparent's home, or a friend's house. Many medications are never finished and are stored in bathroom medicine cabinets or left on top of refrigerators or kitchen cabinets. All of these methods of storage allow kids easy access to prescription drugs. Kids may not even know what drugs they are consuming but are merely experimenting. Others know exactly the type of drugs they are searching for and may only take a few pills out of a bottle at a time so as not to raise suspicion. Kids will also take pills from several different bottles and ingest them all at one time, which is commonly known as "pharming."

Grandparents are also easy prey as they usually have numerous medications, and if some pills are missing, it is simply overlooked as grandma or grandpa forgot and took or misplaced the pills.

It is not uncommon for individuals to obtain medications through some type of criminal activity. Burglarizing pharmacies and veterinarian clinics allows access to large amounts of controlled substances; however, the fear of arrest deters many of them.

Once pills are obtained, kids will now try to conceal them in several different ways including mixing the prescription pills with over-the-counter drugs like Tylenol or Advil. If the pills are oval in shape, the center is drilled out and are then placed on a candy necklace and worn around the neck to be taken anytime in front of anyone. If you find pills in your child's possession, whether it is in their room, duffel bags, cars, or on their person, the first step is to question what the pills are and the use for them. The next thing to do is confirm the story. If they say they are a friend's pills, obtain the friend's name and call his or her parents and ask if the friend is taking any medication and tell the parents why you are asking. A large majority of parents are concerned for the welfare of their children's friends and will want to help in any way they can.

If you are not able to obtain that information, the next step is to call the local pharmacy or hospital and describe the pill or go to WebMD@www.webmd.com. You can also call the nationwide Poison Control Center at 1-800-222-1222, which has personnel available twenty-four-hours-a-day, seven-days-a-week. The center will generally have the ability to provide information about the pill that you have located. You will have to describe the pill including the color, shape, design, size and any numbers or letters engraved on it. Prescription medications are usually identifiable within a short time. The center can also provide you with information regarding the schedule of the drug and the physical signs and symptoms a person displays while under the influence of the drug. They can also furnish the overdose signs and symptoms. This will aid in confirming your child's story and provide valuable information. However, the hospitals, pharmacies, and Poison Control Centers will rarely be able to identify pills or capsules like ecstasy, PCP, MDA, PMA (which we will discuss later), and many others which are produced in clandestine labs.

Methods of Ingestion

The most common method of ingesting pills is to orally consume them, however, digestive enzymes in the stomach break down the pills losing some of the potency. Another method of ingestion is to insert the pills rectally or dissolve the pills in water placing them in an enema bottle for insertion. These methods bypass the stomach acids allowing for rapid absorption of the drug. This is commonly referred to among users as "bum nuts." Pills that are water soluble can also be crushed or ground up and then snorted. If you locate any of the following items—hypodermic needles, spoons, the bottoms of soda cans, bottle caps, a piece of rubber, a belt, shoe string, cotton balls the size of peas, or the tip of a filtered cigarette—they are indicative of someone injecting drugs.

The individual will crush the pills, place the substance onto a spoon, bottle cap, or the bottom of a soda can, and add a small amount of water on top of the crushed substance. Cotton balls or the tips of a filtered cigarette are placed onto the substance. The user then places the tip of the needle on top of the cotton ball or piece of cigarette filter and draws up the substance through the cotton and into the hypodermic needle. Unlike street drugs, prescription medications do not need to be "cooked up" or heated up because there are no impurities. The reason the cotton balls or the cigarette filter tips are used is because binders contained within the medication can clog the hypodermic needle. This method also bypasses the stomach providing a direct route into the bloodstream and to the brain. Like with any drug that individuals inject, locations vary depending on personal preferences and the length of time they have been injecting. A majority of people inject into the crook of the arm as they are some of the easiest veins to locate. As we continue to inject into these veins they begin to collapse making them more difficult to use. Users then find other places to inject that can consist of veins under the tongue, under toenails and fingernails, feet, behind the knee, and even in the genitals.

Red Flags for Parents

You should take note of pill bottles with multiple medications contained within, pill bottles with the label removed or the label lists the name of a different person. Also look for grinders or pill crushers which will powderize the pills, hypodermic needles, spoons, the bottoms of soda cans, bottle caps, a piece of rubber, a belt, shoe string, many cotton balls the size of peas or the tip of a filtered cigarette. Take note of your child wearing long sleeve clothing, especially in warm weather, to cover up injection sites or bruising. T-shirts with logos of drug slang terms and musical bands that promote drug use are popular with users. One of the new trends is to wear an "Orange Crush" T-shirt, because among much of today's youth, it stands for crushing pills.

Rohypnol

Rohypnol, or roofies, is a powerful sedative depressant estimated to be ten times stronger than Valium. Since it is illegal in the United States but is legal in over seventy countries, rohypnol is smuggled in from Mexico and is more prevalent in southwestern states. It is also a drug of concern in connection to sexual assaults, as tablets are crushed up and placed into unsuspecting victim's drinks. Rohypnol has no odor or taste, but the manufacturer has added dyes to the tablets so individuals can see color differences in their drinks. However, dark colored drinks make it much more difficult to observe the color change from the dye.

The effects begin within fifteen to thirty minutes after consumption and can last for up to sixteen hours depending upon the dose taken. The drug causes amnesia effects where the victim cannot recall events, hence, a drug of choice for sexual predators. Rohypnol is not as commonly used in sexual assaults as GHB, because it is detectable for up to seventy-two hours in the victim's urine.

GHB is Gamma-Hydroxybutyrate and is often referred to as "the date rape drug" (a popular media term, but more appropriately just "rape drug" or "predatory drug") replacing rohypnol in many areas of the country. GHB is produced in clandestine laboratories with the recipe readily available on the Internet. GHB can be a liquid or powder; it can also be odorless, colorless, and somewhat tasteless, but it can also have a chemical odor, a salty taste, and be disguised with a wide variety of colors. The effects of GHB vary greatly depending on the purity and the amount ingested. One to two grams generally cause relaxation, reduced inhibitions, amnesia, and a general feeling much like alcohol intoxification. Two to five grams can cause motor coordination difficulties, unarousable sleep, or even coma. As each person is different, it is difficult to estimate how much of the drug a person could ingest without severe medical complications. This is a very dangerous drug, and with a variance of only a few grams, may result in coma or death.

GHB has become a drug of choice by sexual predators that have accessed over 40 plus drugs to facilitate sexual assaults. Adding about a capful of GHB to an unsuspecting victim's drink can render them in a blackout state or even comatose *(photo 5.8, 5.9)*. Case in point would be the heir to the Max Factor family fortune, Andrew Luster, who drugged women with GHB and then sexually assaulted them. He was later convicted of 86 criminal charges and sentenced to 124 years in prison.

GHB can also be frozen in ice cubes and mixed into a person's drink. As the person consumes the beverage and the ice cubes melt, the victim begins to consume the GHB. The victim fades into amnesia or unconsciousness and is sexually assaulted with little knowledge or recollection of the attack. This crime happens across the country to both males and females at bars, parties, high school dances, and underage drinking parties.

The effects of GHB include amnesia, disorientation, and cataplexy, which is a complete loss of muscle control, and are accommodating for sexual assaults. Some victims will never know an assault took place, while others will begin to have vivid partial recollections of an assault. However, by then too much time may have passed to capture GHB in testing, but a sexual assault kit should be completed at a hospital anyway, in case other longer lasting drugs were actually administered. GHB is only detectable for approximately four hours in the blood and twelve hours in the urine. The rapid elimination of the drug from the body makes it very difficult to detect. Most officers in law enforcement are unaware of the constringent time limits to obtain a positive test result from the victim. If you suspect GHB in a sexual assault of your child, immediately seek medical assistance for the proper tests. Because most hospital labs are unable to test for GHB and doctors may not recognize the symptoms, you should request an extra urine sample. Then if needed, the urine could be sent to the state crime lab for further testing.

GHB is also ingested recreationally for its intoxicating effects at high school dances, teen dance clubs, or at raves and can be more popular than alcohol as it is far less detectable. Kids cannot walk into a dance carrying a can of beer or a bottle of alcohol but can carry in a water bottle or sports drink *(photo 5.10)*. Unknown to the chaperons the water bottle or sports drink may contain a few grams of GHB mixed with the liquid. Typically when someone is dancing throughout the night and they become thirsty, they normally leave the dance floor and gulp down water. If you notice individuals dancing and repeatedly leaving the dance floor to take a few small sips from a water bottle, and then return to dancing and return to the water bottle a short time later, again taking small sips they are probably dosing themselves with GHB. The user knows if they drink the entire bottle at once, it could cause them to become unconscious.

It is also possible for individuals who are simply dosing themselves to consume too much GHB and render themselves unconscious. In cases where there are no chaperones available, it is not unheard of for an individual who consumed GHB to collapse on the dance floor in an unconscious or semiconscious state. The party will continue with little or no concern for the safety of those affected by the drug. There are known incidents at raves where security personnel or friends have dragged the unconscious person to the corner of the room where they are left to lay as the party continues. Kids have died in this state from aspirating on their own vomit. Others have died because an overdose state lowers pulse, blood pressure, and respiration slowing the body down to a point where it cannot return to homeostasis.

To determine if GHB is contained in a water bottle, shake it vigorously. If the water becomes cloudy or foams, some chemical, probably GHB, has been added to the water *(photo 5.11)*. If you shake a water bottle containing only water, the color does not change and the bubbles that form dissipate rapidly. Shaking the bottle next to a bottle that is known to be pure water is a good idea for comparison purposes.

It should be noted that this test only works with pure water, as there are several drinks available on the market that when shaken actually foam because of carbonation and other chemicals but do not contain GHB.

GHB is typically not placed in Styrofoam cups as the chemicals will destroy the bottoms of the cups. If you are cleaning up from a party, take note of these indicators of possible drug activity.

So why is GHB so hard to identify? GHB is difficult to identify, because it can be added to so many different products. Visine bottles, soda, water, ice cubes, or anything containing a liquid can contain GHB; food coloring can also be added to change the color of a drink, again, making visual identification difficult. One thing to look for is bottles with the labels worn off. An example is a Visine bottle typically used to get the red out of bloodshot eyes. Drug users or sexual predators will simply keep refilling the bottle with liquid GHB, and over time the label will wear off. This happens because when refilling the bottle the chemicals coming in contact with the outside of the container deface or destroy the label. Again, simply shaking a bottle of Visine will cause the Visine to foam; it is the fact that the label is missing that should cause a red flag.

Athletes, especially weight lifters and body builders, also abuse GHB for its deep sleep effects. Many body builders believe that muscle growth occurs best during REM, or stage four deep sleep. Therefore, if a weight lifter schedules his workouts around the ingestion of GHB, he believes he will become bigger faster. An example of a possible scenario is during summertime and the high school gym is open for the football players to work out. A player arrives at the gym and does an hour workout. He returns home and takes a small dose of GHB and sleeps for about three to four hours. He then gets up and goes back to the gym for a second workout, or what is known as a "split workout." This would allow for two workouts and recovery time in between. In his mind, he believes that his body would recover and grow faster because of the deep sleep between his workouts. There is no research that confirms that GHB promotes muscle growth, since sleeping under its influence causes a temporary, minute spike in growth hormone production, and thus, is not anabolic.

Medical Purpose

GHB is currently a schedule I and II drug, which means it has some medical applications in the United States, and is currently prescribed under the trade name Xyrem. It is tightly restricted and is prescribed to individuals with narcolepsy and those who experience episodes of loss of muscle control known as cataplexy. Xyrem is to be taken at bedtime with a second dose taken a few hours later. This is supposed to allow a person who has narcolepsy and cataplexy to obtain deep sleep which may provide them with fewer episodes of falling asleep the next day. People with this disease will probably also continue to take medications that are stimulants to assist them in staying awake during the daytime hours. It is also being prescribed in "off label" use for some with fibromyalgia; it is not officially approved for that use. Patients on Xyrem may experience some of the same problems abusers of rape victim's experience, such as sleepwalking and loss of bladder or fecal control.

Methods of Ingestion

Normally GHB is ingested by mixing it with a beverage, or it can also be consumed orally without anything added or by capsule. However, another method of ingestion is to soak a tampon in liquid GHB and insert it rectally, this is commonly known as "tea-bag-ging" *(photo 5.12)*. The GHB goes directly into the bloodstream bypassing the stomach. Users then may have a friend remove the tampon after becoming unconscious.

Products Containing GHB, GBL, or Analogs of GHB

Believe it or not, there are hundreds of products on the market today that contain GHB, GBL (gamma-Butyrolactone), 1,4-butanediol, gamma-Valerolactone or other analogs or chemical cousins, some legal for industrial use (but not for human consumption) and some merely disguised as "products" in an effort to evade prosecution. There are some products on the commercial market that contain both GHB and GBL. Some products that contain GBL are nail polish removers, engine degreasers, paint strippers, and other cleaners. Drug pushers will also make phony products, disguising them as cleaning products such as inkjet printer cleaners, but actually sell them knowing that they are being ingested. If the products contain gamma-Butyrolactone, 1,4-butanediol, example Somax organic cleaning solution *(photo 5.13)* they metabolize into GHB when consumed. Because many of these chemicals are not intended for human consumption, some are used as a precursor to create GHB or are merely consumed on their own as they either convert to GHB in the body or at least produce comparable effects. Many individuals are not concerned with the additional chemicals contained within the various "legitimate" products and consume them anyway.

Here are a few examples Once Removed Nail Polish Remover *(photo 5.14)* contains butyrolactone (gamma-Butyrolactone), which when ingested metabolizes into GHB in our bodies. And yes, kids were drinking this. I say "were" drinking this, because since this book has been written, Once Removed Nail Polish has stopped using butyrolactone as an ingredient. That just goes to show that kids are well aware of the ingredients manufacturers use and which ones will produce effects similar to GHB.

Mavala non-acetone nail polish remover pads also contain butyrolactone and are placed in the mouth and sucked on for the effects or dropped into drink containers. Sally's Nail Polish Remover, Sally's 5 Second Nails, and Helping Hand Super Glue Remover are all legitimate products that once contained butyrolactone.

It is hard to imagine kids drinking these chemicals, but addiction can cause people to do things they would not normally do. Whether the addiction is psychological or physical, it doesn't matter—the damage to the brain and body may be irreversible.

Red Flags for Parents

Red flags for parents are any items including bumper stickers, T-shirts, hats, scribbling on folders and notebooks, posters, or knickknacks with terms like GHB, "G," Georgia Home Boy, Gina (common in the gym scene), Grievous Bodily Harm, easy lay, Liquid X, Liquid E, Gamma 10, Scoop, Swirl, Geed-up, Geed-out, Gib, Cherry Meth, Salty Water, Soap Jib, Fantasy, and Women's Viagra.

Remember to shake water bottles to see if they foam or become cloudy. Smell the contents, checking for a chemical odor. If your kids go to parties, talk to them about never leaving their drink unattended and the dangers of drug-facilitated sexual assaults. In addition, look for tampons, nail polish remover or nail polish, especially if located in a male's bedroom or hidden in pockets in his clothing. Most guys will not carry feminine products for their girlfriends. Look at the labels of the products to see if they contain GHB or any of its analogs.

Homeopathic Drugs

Homeopathic substances like valerian root *(photo 5.15)* and kava kava are also drugs that cause mild to heavy sedation, depending on the dose taken. Valeric acid is a liquid available over the internet and is advertised to reduce stress, fight insomnia, and help in

40

post-workout recovery. It is a colorless liquid with an unpleasant odor much like sweat. These products are legal and are advertised as natural sleep aids. Solar water is sold on the internet and arrives at your doorstep as a white powder and can be mixed with your favorite beverage. The product contains chemicals that will again cause mild to heavy sedation. There are numerous other products on the market advertised as natural sleep aids, but impairment occurs when these substances are taken at abuse levels.

Renwetrient is another sedating drug advertised as a natural sleep aid not containing GHB but does contain GBL. As stated earlier GBL converts in our bodies into GHB *(photo 5.16)*.

Physical Signs Associated with Depressants

Generally, depressants will not affect body temperature; however, they will lower pulse and blood pressure. One exception is the fact that alcohol can elevate a person's pulse. A person will also become uncoordinated, have difficulty with their gait, displaying a rubber-legged appearance. You may also observe disorientation, drowsiness, amnesia, thick slurred speech, droopy eyes, vomiting, drunk-like behavior, fumbling, body tremors, unconsciousness or coma. If alcohol had been consumed, an odor of intoxicants will also be present.

Street Terminology

Gamma-hydroxybutyrate	Over-the-Counter	Prescription
GHB	Robo	Downers
Gib	Tussin	Barbs
Scoop	Going Robo	Doors
Easy Lay	Sipping Syrup	Reds
Women's Viagra	Sylum	Yellow Jackets
Liquid X	CCC	Loads
Salty Water	DXM	Ludes
Vita-G	Skittels	Soaps
Cap	Skittling	Blues
Goop	Orange Drink	Mickey Finn
Grievous Bodily Harm	O.J.	Pink Ladies
Georgia Home Boy		714's
Great Hormones at Bedtime		Rainbows
Water		Da-bul
Liquid ecstasy		
Gamma		
GBH		
Gamma-o		
Fantasy		
G-riffic		
Cherry Meth		
Sleep		

Rohypnol
Rophies
Ropes
Forget Me Pill
Mexican Valium
Circles
Ruffies
Mind Eraser
Roofies

CHAPTER 6

Stimulants

Stimulants affect the body in a predictable fashion. It does not matter what the type of drug ingested is, whether it is cocaine, methamphetamine, prescription medications like Ritalin, or amphetamines, the physical signs will generally be the same. Stimulants will cause excitement, talkativeness, body tremors, alertness, weight loss, elevated pulse and blood pressure, and a general sense of high energy. There are various types of stimulants, some of which are legal and some illegal. Legal stimulants include caffeine, energy drinks such as Red Bull, Monster Energy Drink, NOS, and energy pills like Yellow Jackets, 357 Magnum, PEPTIME, Xtreme PEPTIME, and prescribed medications such as Ritalin and Adderall. Among the illegal substances are cocaine, crack, rock, freebase cocaine, methamphetamine, khat, Methcathinone, and numerous others.

Amphetamines

Amphetamines have many legal uses in the medical field and are prescribed to treat a variety of disorders including narcolepsy, Parkinson's disease, obesity, ADD and ADHD. Ritalin and Adderall are medications prescribed to individuals diagnosed with attention deficit hyperactivity disorder (ADHD), and attention deficit disorder (ADD). Even though Ritalin and Adderall are stimulants, when prescribed to individuals diagnosed with ADHD and ADD, they have a calming effect allowing these individuals to function more normally. What unfortunately happens is these drugs end up in the hands of individuals who do not need the medication and the effects now mimic the signs and symptoms of someone under the influence of a stimulant. The pills can be taken orally or crushed up and snorted giving the user similar effects to that of cocaine. If the medication is water soluble, it can be dissolved in water and then injected. Again, if pills are located, contact your local pharmacy, hospital, or the Poison Control Center at 1-800-222-1222 to determine what the pills are.

Energy Drinks and Pills

Energy drinks or energy pills, which many of us consume, are also used by kids to perform better in athletics and academics. The problem with those drinks or pills is the large amount of caffeine, ephedra, or other herbs they contain. Let's look at the chemicals in Red Bull, a popular energy drink. One 12-ounce can of Coca-Cola contains about 34 milligrams of caffeine; one 8.5-ounce can of Red Bull contains 80 milligrams of caffeine, about three times the amount of that in the can of Coke. Red Bull also contains the following ingredients; 1000 milligrams of taurine a nonessential amino acid; 600 milligrams of glucuronolactone, which is basically a carbohydrate but is two times the recommended daily dose; vitamin B6, which is needed to process the taurine; approximately 5 spoonfuls of sucrose and glucose, which is sugar; aspartame/sucralose, which is a sweetener/preservative which many pregnant women are advised to stay away from; and acesulfame K, a sugar substitute with carcinogenic potential. Countries like Australia and Canada have removed many of the energy drinks from the shelves of stores because of health issues associated with the products *(photo 6.1)*.

In a DRE class that I was instructing, a student volunteered to drink a can of Red Bull. While he sat in front of the class, his pulse elevated from 70 beats per minute to 130 beats per minute in about 5 minutes.

Now imagine your son or daughter participating in an athletic event; they are physically active and their heart is already working at its maximum. This is where the problem arises. They become tired and now ingest an energy drink or energy pills. Their heart, which is naturally accelerated from exercise, is now stimulated to work even harder, putting them in danger of cardiac arrest.

Ephedra is another stimulant found in various herbal drugs and, until recently, was legal. However, it is still sold in products under different names like Ma Huhug, a Chinese herb. These drugs elevate pulse, blood pressure, and temperature with sometimes disastrous results.

As you make a purchase at the local convenience store, try to observe all of the different types of energy pills available. The concept behind the pills is the same as the energy drinks, increased alertness along with elevating the body's normal regulators.

Ginseng, ginkgo biloba, ginger and garlic may be advertised as being one or more of the ingredients in the products. However, it does not inform you that these substances also thin the blood. Individuals with heart problems or who may be going in for surgery or even to have a tooth pulled could put themselves in danger, as the doctor or dentist may have a difficult time stopping the bleeding should a medical emergency occur.

Cat Candy or Catnip, the treat given to cats, is also being abused by humans for its stimulating effects. Catnip is being smoked, chewed, and even mixed with marijuana cigarettes *(photo 6.2)*.

Plants

Khat is a plant grown primarily in Africa and the active ingredient is cathanone, which is a schedule 1 drug in the United States. As the khat plant dries, it loses its potency and the cathanone is destroyed leaving cathine, a schedule IV drug. The leaves of the plant can be chewed, brewed in a tea, or cooked as a food giving it a stimulant type of effect *(photo 6.3)*. The practice of chewing on the leaves is common among the Somali, Ethiopian, and Yemeni cultures. Like other stimulants, khat initially gives the user increased energy, and causes appetite suppression and hyperactivity. The effects generally last between two and three hours. Frequent use of the drug can mimic the effects of cocaine and methamphetamine, causing paranoia, psychosis, schizophrenia, and hallucination.

Cocaine

Cocaine is derived from the coca plant usually grown in Columbia. It takes about 200 to 300 pounds of coca leaves to make about one pound of cocaine. Cocaine is usually a white powdery substance; however, recently, black cocaine has been located by several law enforcement agencies across the country. The cocaine was dyed a different color to thwart law enforcement. Cocaine can also be somewhat chunky, generally depending on how many times it has been "cut." An example of the term "cut" is if a person has 5 grams of cocaine and they add a white powder of similar consistency, such as baking soda, ground up vitamin B tablets, inositol (a dietary supplement), or mannitol (baby laxative), they can increase the amount of grams and enhance their profit. Powder cocaine is ingested through the nose or it may be injected. Continually snorting cocaine through the nose eventually causes a deterioration of the septum, and a hole forms between the nostrils. Abusers also suffer from runny or bloody noses, along with chronic sinus problems. Sometimes residue of white powder can also be observed under the nose or even in the nostrils, as users forget to wipe their nose after ingestion of the drug. When snorting, the effects last about five to ninety minutes depending on how much was ingested and the quality of the cocaine.

Small amounts, usually a gram, are stored in what is referred to as a "bindle." A bindle is high gloss paper folded multiple times into the shape of a rectangle. The ink in high gloss paper will not absorb into the cocaine, so it will not be tainted. Another reason high gloss paper is chosen is that the powdered cocaine will not stick to the paper and can be removed easily. Plastic sandwich baggies are also used to package cocaine *(photo 6.4)*. The amount can range from several ounces to a few grams. An amount of cocaine is placed into the corner of the plastic baggie; it is then twisted, knotted, and the remainder of the bag is disposed of. The cost of a gram of cocaine is approximately $100 and yields twenty to thirty one-inch lines *(photo 6.5)*.

If you believe it is impossible for your child to use drugs without your knowledge, the following is a true life example. I was teaching a class in Arizona and one of the test subjects was an eighteen-year-old female, who had been ingesting cocaine since she was thirteen, unbeknownst to her parents. As I looked in her nose, I could clearly see a hole about the size of the tip of your pinky going from one side of the septum to the other. She used cocaine for six years with her parents never seeing the signs of drug use.

Methods of Ingestion

Injecting cocaine and other drugs is another method of ingestion that also creates health concerns. While the majority of abusers choose to inject in a vein, some inject intramuscularly, which means into the muscle, and still others will inject directly into the carotid artery in the neck. Users commonly share dirty needles, which can lead to the spread of disease, infection, and even gangrene. The most common place to inject is in the veins of the arms and legs, as veins are easier to find. As addicts continue to inject in the same area, the veins collapse leaving what is referred to as "track marks" behind. Track marks are scars that develop after continued injections in the same area. One inch of track marks equals approximately 50 to 100 injections. It is not uncommon for users to inject between the fingers and toes, under fingernails and toenails, in the neck, and in tattoos in an attempt to hide the injection marks. Users also inject in what is referred to as the "sweet spot." This is an area that is only injected into on rare occasions. The sweet spot is usually in the veins under the tongue or in the penis or vagina. Cocaine powder is also dissolved in water and a razor blade is used to cut open a vein at which time the liquid cocaine is squirted into the open wound.

Generally, razor blades and mirrors are common among users who snort cocaine by placing the cocaine on a mirror and then use a razor blade to divide it into lines for snorting *(photo 6.6)*. Straws referred to as "tooters" have been cut down to an approximate length of two to four inches and are used to snort cocaine *(photo 6.7)*. Many users actually pierce their ears and then slowly increase the size of the hole to accommodate the straw. They then carry the straw they use for snorting around in the hole in their ear. Spoons smaller than baby spoons are also used by placing cocaine in the spoon, which is then held up to the nose and the cocaine snorted. "Bullets" are another device used to ingest cocaine; they are usually plastic cylindrical devices. Each bullet can hold several grams of cocaine and a valve allows certain amounts into the tip for ingestion *(photo 6.8)*.

Red Flags for Parents

Terms like coke, cola, snow, powder, toot and blow are common among powdered cocaine users. Look for plastic baggies containing white powder or a residue of white powder, plastic baggies with the corners cut or pulled off, and small plastic knots. Be aware of high glossy papers folded into small rectangles known as bindles and very small spoons, which are also used to ingest powdered cocaine. Look at the pinky finger and note if the fingernail is obviously longer than the other nails. Cocaine is often placed on the nail and placed in the nose. Simply looking for white powder residue is an easy observation, too. Also look at a person's earlobe for a hole the size of a straw. Users may carry the straw they use for snorting in the hole in their ear.

Crack Cocaine

Crack, rock, and freebase cocaine are different recipes for base cocaine. Base cocaine is basically a hardened form of powdered cocaine. The color can vary from white to off white or even black. The difference between each form of base cocaine is the recipe that was used to make it. Each recipe causes a chemical reaction, which turns the powder into a smokable form. Crack cocaine is about 19 to 33 percent pure cocaine, while "rock" cocaine is about 50 to 60 percent pure cocaine, and freebase cocaine is about 90 to 95 percent pure. It doesn't matter which form of base cocaine was purchased, the finished product all looks the same. The reason there is a variation in the purity is the amount of adulterants added to the powdered cocaine during the process of changing it to base cocaine. We will just refer to all base cocaine as "crack" for simplicity. If a person starts with one ounce of powdered cocaine and uses the crack cocaine recipe, the finished product would yield about three ounces of crack. The only purpose to alter the powdered cocaine to crack cocaine is so it can be smoked. Once cocaine has been changed to crack, it is no longer water soluble and cannot be injected or snorted.

So where does the term "crack" come from? It actually got its name from the crackling sound it makes when it is heated and smoked. When produced, crack rocks can be larger than a bar of soap. However, the crack is broken down to approximately the size of a pea for sale to users. Since the crack rocks are very small in size, they are easily concealed *(photo 6.9, 6.10, 6.11)*.

The crack rocks are normally packaged in the corners of plastic sandwich baggies. The corners are then twisted with the rock inside and tied into a knot. When a person purchases these rocks they will generally pull the rock from its plastic wrapper, tossing the small plastic knot aside. Crack rocks are also placed in the bottoms of cigarette cellophane wrappers and inside of tinfoil gum wrappers *(photo 6.12)*.

In some areas of the country, it is easier to obtain crack cocaine than it is to obtain cocaine powder. Because users generally prefer a specific method of ingestion, a process to change crack cocaine back into a powdered form was developed. Acetone is added to the crack cocaine which then crystallizes, leaving a powder that can be snorted or injected.

Methods of Ingestion

For smoking, the user can use elaborate glass pipes, *(photo 6.13)* but generally they use copper or metal tubes *(photo 6.14)*. Even broken off antennas from automobiles can be used as a pipe to ingest crack cocaine. One of the telltale signs of uncovering a crack pipe is by looking inside the tube. Look to see if there are burned or discolored pieces of Chore Boy Scrubbers contained within the tube. Chore Boy is like S.O.S soap pads but without the chemicals *(photo*

6.15). If Chore Boy is observed, you have found a crack pipe. The purpose of the Chore Boy is to hold the crack rock in place while smoking it. Users also wrap the middle and end of the pipe with duct tape or electrical tape, because the pipe becomes extremely hot causing the lips and fingertips to burn. The tape provides a barrier protecting the finger tips and lips from the intense heat.

Have you ever been to a gas station and noticed fresh roses in the garbage minus the glass tube from the bottom of the stems that contained the water? That's because what is missing is a 99 cent crack pipe. Users typically purchase the roses and throw them out only to keep the glass vial and use it for a crack pipe. Crack cocaine is placed into the bottom with Chore Boy, heated, and then inhaled. Chronic base cocaine smokers will generally have a charred or almost melted appearance to their fingertips. Their lips may also become dried and cracked.

The onset of the high from smoking crack cocaine is immediate and lasts only about ten to fifteen minutes leaving the user craving another rock. Crack rocks vary in cost depending on size, but are generally between $20 and $40.

Many kids purchase marijuana cigarettes without knowing that small pieces of crack cocaine have been laced in with the marijuana. After smoking the marijuana cigarette, they can potentially become hooked on crack cocaine.

Red Flags for Parents

Baking soda is the most common method to convert powdered cocaine to crack cocaine *(photo 6.16)*. Household products like vitamins, baby laxatives, baking powder, inositol, mannitol, vitamin B, or basically any powdered product which is white in color are added to powdered cocaine to increase the amount of the product. Crack cocaine is generally concealed in the corner of a plastic baggie. Look for baggies that have been pulled apart or very small plastic knots from the corner of where the crack had been placed. Paraphernalia associated with crack cocaine includes mini-blowtorch lighters along with glass and metal pipes with Chore Boy inside. Crown Royal bags are also a common place to store crack or marijuana pipes *(photo 6.17)*. When in your child's room or vehicle look for pieces of Chore Boy on the seats or floor mats *(photo 6.18)*. As users pull pieces of Chore Boy off of the pad, small strands fall to the floor of the car or bedroom sticking to fibers in the carpet.

Because these drugs burn at high temperatures, physical signs on the body will develop with continued use. As a user continues to hold onto glass or metal pipes, their fingertips become charred or even take on a melted appearance *(photo 6.19a, 6.19b)*. When the pipe is continually placed to the lips for ingestion, the lips also become cracked or even discolored. Many users carry lip balm or ChapStick for their lips. The enamel on teeth deteriorates and teeth may break or become ground down from constant teeth grinding. For certain individuals histamines released into the body cause a type of allergic reaction where they begin to itch or pick at their skin, generally on the arms, neck, chest, or face. This occurrence is known among users as "snow bugs," as many feel there are actually bugs crawling on their skin. Some users even hallucinate, actually seeing the bugs *(photo 6.20a, 6.20b)*.

Methcathinone

Methcathinone is very similar to methamphetamine. It first appeared in Upper Michigan in the 1990s and was popular for a few years but never really caught on and popularity has decreased. The physical effects are very much like any of the stimulants being abused.

Methamphetamine

In the 1960s and 1970s, outlaw motorcycle gangs like the Hells Angels and Outlaws controlled much of the methamphetamine market. Today much of the market is controlled by Mexican gangs, who produce the largest amounts of methamphetamine and smuggle it into the United States. Because large amounts are produced at one time it reduces the cost, which allows for cheaper prices, especially for states that border Mexico.

Methamphetamine is also produced in clandestine laboratories across our country with well over 150 different manufacturing variations available on the internet. Have you ever gone to the local store and seen a sign indicating a maximum of three boxes of pseudoephedrine for sale to any one individual at one time? The purpose of this is to curb the production of methamphetamine, because pseudoephedrine is one of the main ingredients. However, the law doesn't really work, as users can just go to several different stores and continue to purchase the boxes of pseudoephedrine until they obtain the desired amount. Multiple users can also go into a store at the same time and each purchase three boxes, combine their amounts, and begin the production of methamphetamine.

As previously mentioned, there are well over 150 ways to produce methamphetamine and I will not give any of the recipes in this book, but will simply state that they are easily obtainable via the internet. The cooking of methamphetamine is extremely dangerous because chemicals used in the production are extremely volatile and unstable. Labs are located anywhere—in country settings, city houses, storage sheds, hotel rooms; the list is endless. Think about that the next time you check into a hotel room or are buying a house where a meth lab could have been. The chemicals are absorbed into the walls, carpets, furniture, and upon contact or prolonged exposure can cause severe illness. Labs across the country have exploded killing innocent people including children. Labs also produce large amounts of hazardous waste, which are disposed of in parks, ditches, fields, and woods—basically anywhere.

What is the physical addiction to meth? A methamphetamine user has been known to stay awake for days without sleep. This is commonly referred to as "Tweeking" and the user is known as a "Tweeker." As the user ingests methamphetamine over the course of several days, their body crashes and they will sleep for a number of days or even a week. Bodily functions, however, continue to occur, and when users awaken, they have urinated, defecated, or vomited on themselves. Like with all drugs, over the course of time, users develop a tolerance and require larger and larger amounts of the drug to continue to achieve the same effects.

If you still believe your child will not be affected by these drugs, I had the opportunity to speak with a twenty-year-old female, who informed me she had been using methamphetamine since she was eleven years old and that her parents never used drugs. However, the neighbor who lived next door cooked methamphetamine and provided it to her starting at age eleven. She stated her parents never caught on. I asked her if she could do her life over again and not use drugs, would she. Her response was mind-boggling. She stated, "No, I would do it all again, because that is how I met my old man and he gave me my babies." I asked how many children she had and she stated four with one on the way. I asked why she would put her child's health at risk and use drugs during pregnancy. She stated that using methamphetamine while pregnant made the kids faster and smarter, because they grow faster from the drug. She also stated that when she had not used drugs during pregnancy, those children were not as smart.

As individuals become more addicted to the drug, their physical well being becomes less of a concern as the drug begins to control their lives. A large majority of users lose body weight, because stimulants like methamphetamine and cocaine are appetite suppressants. I spoke with one young man who moved from West Virginia to Phoenix, Arizona, and began using methamphetamine. In a year's time he went from 260 pounds to 160 pounds, losing 100 pounds in one year. He had never had contact with law enforcement while living in West Virginia, and since moving to Phoenix, in a one-year time period, he had been criminally charged with seven misdemeanors and three felonies.

Methods of Ingestion

The common methods to ingest methamphetamine are by snorting, smoking, or injecting, known as slamming. Snorting methamphetamine causes the same physical harm as snorting cocaine; the septum will first become red and ulcerated. As the user continues to ingest drugs by snorting, the septum deteriorates and a small hole begins to form. Continued use will actually cause the hole to keep growing larger until the septum is destroyed.

Glass pipes, which are similar to the ones used to ingest crack cocaine, are again the method usually used to smoke methamphetamine. The pipes are a little different, as Chore Boy is not needed *(photo 6.21)*. Methamphetamine pipes are usually glass with a bulb on the bottom and may have a straight or bent tube. The methamphetamine is placed in the bottom of the pipe where it is then heated; the vapors rise to the top of the pipe where the users inhale the vapors. The pipes may have numerous bends in them where the user can place small amounts of water to help cool the methamphetamine as it is smoked. Powdered methamphetamine can be changed into a hard rock form know as "glass" or "ice." This is done because the hard rock form can be smoked several times before it breaks down.

We have all walked into a room and turned on the light switch and the lights are burned out, right? Concern should arise if the bulbs are actually missing or the filaments are found in the garbage can. Users will remove the filament and wash out the light bulb with soap and water. The light bulb has just been converted into a methamphetamine pipe. The methamphetamine is placed into the bottom of the bulb and then heated. At the same time, the user places their lips around the base inhaling the vapors.

As with crack pipes, methamphetamine pipes burn at hot temperatures, and users often wrap duct tape or electrical tape around the portion they inhale from to keep from burning their lips.

Red Flags for Parents

Unlike ravers, methamphetamine and crack cocaine users do not generally advertise the use of their drugs; they try to hide it. Parents need to look for charred or burnt fingertips. These are telltale signs of drug use, as the pipes used to ingest the drug burn at such high temperatures, it destroys the epidermis on the fingertips. Lips also become dried, cracked, blistered, or even discolored from the pipes used for smoking. The inside of the mouth can have blisters and the enamel on teeth breaks down *(photo 6.22a, 6.22b)*. After your child visits the dentist, ask if anything unusual was noted.

Look for deteriorating hygiene and weight loss, meth bugs or skin picking *(photo 6.23a, 6.23b, 6.23c)* as this is common among individuals who become addicted to methamphetamine.

The paraphernalia associated with smoking methamphetamine generally consists of glass pipes or light bulbs. If it is injected, look for hypodermic needles, mini pea-sized cotton balls, tips of filtered cigarettes, spoons and bottle caps. Be aware that the process of manufacturing methamphetamine results in various colors of the powdery substance, which may be packaged in plastic sandwich baggies or glass vials.

Physical Signs Associated with Stimulant Use

The following is a list of common side effects of stimulant abuse: elevated pulse, blood pressure, and body temperature *(photo 6.24)*; dilated pupils; cracked lips; charred fingertips; agitation; paranoia; hallucination; grinding of teeth; rotten teeth; mood swings; weight loss; poor hygiene; rapid movements; inability to concentrate; restlessness; excitement; insomnia; dry mouth; runny nose; talkative; increased alertness; redness or ulcerations to nasal area; and inability to obtain erection.

Street Terminology		
Cocaine and Crack	**Methamphetamine**	**Prescription**
Coke	Meth	Black Mollies
Cola	Speed	Leapers
Powder	Glass	Skittles
Flake	Crank	Thrusters
Rock	Ice	Co-pilots
Toot	Crystal	P
Blow	Shake N Bake	Phet
Nose Candy	Glass Booya	Billy
Snow	Crystal Meth	Whizz
Big C	Batu	Sulph
Lady	Tweek	Wake-up
Snowbirds	G	Dex
White	Shabu	Uppers
Girl	Speed	
Uptown	LA Glass	
Chick	LA Ice	
Bernice	Wire	

Over-the-Counter	
*Color of Pills	Yellow Swarm
Blacks	Yellow Bullet
Reds	Power Drive
Yellows	Midnight Stallion
Yellow Jackets (Caffeine)	Thermo Burn
357 Magnum	Red Hotz
8-Hr Energy	Ripped Power
Xtreme PEPTIME	Xtreme Power
Ma Huang	Hundreds of others
Stackers	

CHAPTER 7

Hallucinogens

Hallucinogens are drugs that produce hallucinations. There are basically two types of hallucinogens—natural and synthetic or man-made. Although other drug categories, like depressants, stimulants, and dissociative anesthetics, can at times cause hallucinations, they are generally not taken for their hallucinogenic properties. Hallucinogens cause illusions and delusions. An example would be an illusion is where the person believes they see God. In a delusion the person believes they *are* God.

The following is a list of natural hallucinogens: the Bufo alvarius toad (yes, a live toad), psilocybin mushrooms, San Pedro cactus, peyote (buttons of a certain cactus), nutmeg and mace spices, morning glory flower seeds, jimsonweed, *Salvia divinorum,* and many others.

The synthetic hallucinogens consist of drugs like LSD, MDA, PMA, MDMA or ecstasy, and countless others. There is a debate over whether ecstasy is a stimulant or hallucinogen; for the purposes of this book, it is a hallucinogen with stimulant properties.

Plants

Psilocybin mushrooms are of a particular species of mushroom that cause hallucinations when ingested *(photo 7.1)*. Mushrooms are ingested by smoking, eating them whole or placing them on pizza or other foods, or brewing them into a tea or milkshake. Some users have been known to dip the mushrooms in chocolate disguising them as candies. Studies have identified over one hundred different species of mushrooms with hallucinogenic properties. Amanita muscaria mushrooms are known as "fly agaric" for its ability to attract and kill flies. They are commonly known among users as *Alice in Wonderland* mushrooms and are depicted in fairy tale books or posters. Amanita mushrooms do not contain psilocybin or psilocin but instead contain the hallucinogenic chemicals muscimol and ibotenic acid. This mushroom is related to other deadly mushrooms which look very similar. Ingesting the wrong species of mushrooms can be toxic and kill cells in the liver and kidneys leading to permanent damage to the organs.

Since mushrooms are a naturally occurring fungus, they grow in ditches, in the woods, backyards, and under animal feces. Mushrooms can also be cultivated indoors and are generally grown in a damp, moist area. Oftentimes mushrooms are grown in beverage coolers in damp and dark basements. If your child tells you they are growing mushrooms for a botany project at school, I would have some serious concerns and verify it through the school.

One of the more unusual places users find mushrooms is underneath dried feces of cow, deer, or other animals. Mushrooms are located by flipping over the animal feces; however, they may or may not be of the psilocybin variety. Many poisonous mushrooms resemble the psilocybin variety, and simply choosing the wrong species of mushroom and ingesting it can cause liver and kidney damage resulting in death. Many users believe that simply breaking the stem of the mushroom can reveal whether it is of the psilocybin variety. It is believed that if the mushroom stem turns purple or bluish upon breaking it, it contains psilocin. This may be true in some instances; however, several varieties of poisonous mushrooms also turn color upon breaking the stem.

Mushrooms must be dried prior to bagging or storing them or the chance of spoilage increases. To dry the mushrooms rapidly, they can be placed in an oven at low temperatures, in a microwave oven, or simply placed on a table and dried with a fan or sun lamp.

Magazines like *High Times* and *Grow*, along with numerous internet sites, allow individuals to purchase various species of mushroom spores. Those spores may or may not be of the psilocybin species. Purchasing the spores may or may not be legal depending on the state in which you live, but once you attempt to cultivate the spores, it may become illegal depending on the species of mushroom.

Salvia divinorum is an herb from the family of mint plants that looks like sage and is grown in humid environments, including indoors. The plant contains the chemical salvinorin A, which causes hallucinations. The leaves of the plant are ingested by simply chewing on them, making a tea, or drying the leaves and smoking them. The effects of the drug are much like LSD, however, the effects only last about one hour. The long-term effects of the abuse of salvia are unknown but are believed to be similar to LSD, leaving the user in a psychotic or schizophrenic state. Salvia is legal to possess in most states except in Tennessee, Missouri, Illinois, and several others where legislation has been passed to control it.

I purchased one gram of Salvia divinorum at a head shop (drug shop) in Madison, Wisconsin, for five dollars. When I purchased it, the sales person offered me a liquid extract of salvia stating, "This stuff is better and will blow your mind, and it's legal." Some of the common street terms for salvia are: diviner's sage, sage of the seers, Maria Pastora.

Jimsonweed (the Datura plant) grows wild throughout the United States and is legal to possess. Jimsonweed is abused for its hallucinogenic effects. The plant is ingested by chewing on the leaves or flowers; it can also be brewed into a tea or dried and smoked. The seeds pictured were obtained from a friend who scraped them from plants growing wild in his backyard *(photo 7.2).* Some of the common street terms for jimsonweed are "night shade, angel's trumpet, devil's trumpet, and thorn apple."

Phalaris aquatica is also a plant that grows commonly in the United States, which contains the hallucinogenic chemical DMT. The plant is commonly ingested by smoking it, again brewing it into a tea. Some of the common street terms are "canarygrass, reed canarygrass, and Harding grass".

The peyote cactus grows widely in Mexico and Texas. A few people have the legal right to harvest it for Native Americans, who have legally used the drug for religious purposes for centuries *(photo 7.3).* The cactus has a round top referred to as buttons and contains mescaline, which creates hallucinations. The button or top of the cactus is picked, then dried. It has a bitter taste and can be chewed, smoked, or brewed into an intoxicating drink with the effects lasting up to twelve hours. It can also be ground up and placed in capsules to be swallowed. Do not assume this drug is only being used by Native Americans for religious purposes. In Watertown, Wisconsin, a DRE officer arrested a Caucasian female who ingested mescaline.

The San Pedro cactus is native to Peru and South America and also contains the hallucinogen mescaline. Obtaining the cactus is easier than you think; simply go to the internet where it is readily sold. Now think about the T-shirt you have commonly seen, "Vote for Pedro." Ever wonder what it really means? It can be in reference to the San Pedro cactus.

Since many states do not schedule these common plants, there are no laws regarding their possession. In many states what makes a legal drug illegal is if ingesting it impairs a person's ability to operate a motor vehicle. In other words, to face criminal charges you have to be operating a vehicle while impaired. In some states public intoxification charges may also be applicable; however, most officers will not comprehend the fact that the substance abused is legal. A majority of these substances are not detectable from chemical tests.

Household

The drug culture is certainly willing to experiment. Their experiments have extended into the use of household products. Myristicin is a chemical found in the kitchen spices nutmeg and mace, and when ingested in sufficient quantities, it will give an LSD-type high. Several websites suggest the user consume one tablespoon for every ten pounds of body weight. However, according to numerous individuals who have experimented with nutmeg, much smaller amounts will cause a hallucinogenic experience that can last for several hours, leaving the individual feeling impaired for several days after. If you locate nutmeg or mace in your child's possessions, it should raise some suspicions.

Another surprising substance that kids are experimenting with is the seeds of the morning glory plant, which contains LSA similar to LSD, and when ingested also causes hallucinations *(photo 7.4)*. Users will purchase multiple packs of seeds at home and garden stores. There are usually two methods of ingestion of the seeds. One way is simply eating a large quantity of seeds. The second method is letting the seeds sit in water for several hours. The seeds are removed and the water, which contains chemicals from the seeds that will cause hallucinations, is then consumed. A variation to that is adding the water to other liquids to mask its taste before consuming.

The *Bufo alvarius* toad, which is prevalent to North America, creates venom to protect itself against its predators. The episode of the Simpson's discussed earlier in this book depicts Homer licking a toad; his pupils then dilate and he begins hallucinating. In reality, it is rare to find users actually licking a toad. The toad is captured and squeezed. In an attempt to defend itself, it excretes venom. The venom is then dried and smoked, giving the user an LSD-type experience. The toad can even be ordered off the internet and shipped directly to your home.

There are hundreds of other spices and plants abused for hallucinogenic experiences or stimulating effects. There are too many to list, but websites listed at the end of this book will provide you with a place to start.

Red Flags for Parents

Mushrooms and cactus depicted on hats, T-shirts, wristbands, key chains, and even tattoos can indicate the support of the ingestion of hallucinogenic drugs *(photo 7.5, 7.6)*. Writing or drawings on folders and posters in bedrooms can also be indicative to drug use. Packages of morning glory seeds, bottles of nutmeg or mace spices, film canisters that contain seeds from plants, and plastic baggies containing dried mushrooms are all cause for concern.

Synthetic Drugs and Raves

Raves, which are more recently being advertised as dance parties, techno music parties, teen dances, laser shows, and music festivals are all-night dance parties that are promoted to be alcohol and drug free. During these activities, alcohol and drug free is the furthest thing from the truth, as numerous overdoses and deaths of individuals attending such events have been documented across the country. True ravers have little interest in alcohol, but drugs typically flow freely. Raves are not just held in large cities; they can also be held in empty warehouses, farm fields, and even at an individual's residence. Raves can range from small groups to several hundred to several thousand people. The music being played is usually played by DJs or possibly live bands and generally consists of techno, house, trance, jungle or hip-hop styles. The music is only one facet of a rave and it should not be the concern—the problem is the amount of various drugs being used.

Prior to letting your child attend a "Dance Party," here are some questions to ask that may be helpful in determining the type of activities taking place. What time does the dance party start and end? If your child states they will sleep at a friend's house, be suspicious, as raves often extend into the early morning hours. Check in advance with the friend's parent to be sure this is valid information. Get a specific time they will return from the dance and then follow up with a phone call to that residence. What is the location of the party? How many people will attend? Will medical personnel or security be on hand? Many raves have privately hired medical personnel in an attempt to circumvent the notification of law enforcement of drug-related overdoses. I have been at raves where security has pushed kids out the back door of the event because of their drug-induced state. Security then closes the door and returns to the event, leaving the child lying out on the ground. Next, what type of music will be played? Who is attending? What refreshments are being provided? Remember, kids may leave out specific details regarding the type of party it is. This is your child's life—ask questions!

Ask to see the dance flyer as these often contain clues. Butterflies are the universal symbol of the drug ecstasy and may often appear on the flyers. Flyers may contain graphic characters with pacifiers and dilated pupils, which are also indicators. The letters E or X which may appear highlighted, capitalized, underlined, etc., stand for ecstasy, indicating that the drug will be there.

Young adults will travel great distances to attend a specific rave, especially in communities where there is little else for young people to do. Promoters of raves attempt to create certain elements during the show so that kids will return and tell others about the event. Promoters will provide the most popular music and DJs; they will create astounding light shows that will include the use of laser and strobe lights to enhance the effects of the drugs being ingested.

The ages of those attending raves vary from adolescents through adults. Because many of these club drugs have intoxicating effects, including amnesia and relaxed inhibitions, pedophiles and rapists are also attending raves to take advantage of kids in a drug-induced state. They may or may not be conscious from the drugs' effects but, during this state, their inhibitions are relaxed and they may consent to sexual advances.

Some of the most popular club drugs are GHB, Rohypnol (roofies), methamphetamine, LSD, ketamine, psilocybin mushrooms, DXM (cough syrup), marijuana and numerous others with MDMA (ecstasy) being the most popular. Several of the drugs are both odorless and relatively tasteless, and can be added to someone's beverage without their knowledge increasing the probability for sexual assaults. Even if you believe your child is not abusing drugs or interested in doing so, look at the possibilities of peer pressure with the amount of drugs distributed at a rave. Are you willing to take the chance your child may not return home safely from a dance?

Ecstasy heightens our sense of touch, sight, and hearing. It releases chemicals in our brain called serotonin and dopamine. Serotonin and dopamine are some of our body's chemicals that are produced to help us feel good. Kids are well aware of the massive serotonin release initiated by ecstasy. They also know the initial effects begin within 15–30 minutes with the peak effects occurring at about one hour and the general effects lasting about three to four hours. Kids will consume another ecstasy tablet after the effects of the first pill begin to wear off. This is referred to as "piggy-backing." Robitussin is commonly consumed after the effects of ecstasy wear off, as it is a serotonin reuptake inhibitor, meaning Robitussin will prolong the ecstasy high. Kids may also consume stimulants like ephedrine or methamphetamine or prescription stimulants, such as Ritalin or Adderall, to stay high. What they are unaware of is the fact that when ecstasy causes this large release of serotonin, the cells that produce the serotonin may not reproduce it in the same way afterwards. The cells may grow back haphazardly, reducing the body's ability to produce and process serotonin and dopamine appropriately. What this basically means is eventually we will have a large portion of a generation taking various antidepressants and never feeling normal again.

Ecstasy causes the body temperature to soar to dangerous levels. Because young people refuse to believe this drug can be deadly, they typically do not seek help for their overdosing friends but tell them to drink large quantities of water to cool off or put them into cold showers, baths, or misting rooms thinking this will be adequate. By the time they realize their friends are truly in danger, the damage to the brain from overheating may already have begun.

Another major cause of death among ecstasy users is traffic fatalities. This is because users are up all night long involved in high energy activities. When morning comes around they are very fatigued, yet choose to drive, and many become involved in traffic crashes. Accidents can also occur while still under the influence due to their altered visual perceptions. The ecstasy driver may simply misjudge a turn, for example, and drive off a cliff.

Another sadly common cause of death among ecstasy users is suicide because of the continued loss of serotonin and dopamine and the body's inability to reproduce those chemicals. After continued use of ecstasy, large holes begin to develop in the brain affecting memory, mood, and other brain functions. Recently I purchased a bottle of 5-HPT at a GNC store *(photo 7.7)*. The specific purpose of this product is to assist the body into producing serotonin. Ecstasy users are also aware of this product and combine it with the use of ecstasy in attempt to balance the body's reproduction of serotonin.

What happens at raves? Kids are ingesting various types of drugs. One of the most common is ecstasy, because it heightens the senses and causes several changes to perceptions including vision, touch, and hearing. Ecstasy causes muscle and jaw tension leading to teeth grinding. Kids use pacifiers and mouth guards to alleviate the teeth grinding. Vicks VapoRub is smeared under the eyes or nose and inside of surgical, carpenter, and gas masks opening up bronchial passages and giving the user a cooling sensation *(photo 7.8a, 7.8b)*. The backs of Vicks nasal inhalers are removed and then placed next to a person's eyes, while another person then blows into the inhaler causing a numbing or cooling sensation in the eye.

Glow sticks, spinning toy lights, flashing laser lights are all used at the rave scene. The lights are placed in front of a person's eyes, which cause large light trails and a multitude of colors to be observed *(photo 7.9a, 7.9b)*. The various lights are moved rapidly in front of an individual's eyes, at times overwhelming visual perceptions. No research has been done specifically on the eye issue, but there is a strong possibility that they are doing damage to their eyes because of the dilated pupils caused by ecstasy and the intensity of some of the lights used.

Because our sense of touch is also heightened, vibrating

massagers, plush gloves and gardening gloves with little knobs are commonly used for massaging the upper back, which becomes very tense. They may even have intense muscle spasms though they may not recall them as "painful." It is not uncommon to see guys giving guys back rubs or girls giving girls back rubs. Because of their heightened awareness of their senses, individuals may place their bodies directly against the large speakers that are vibrating from the music. These individuals are known as "speaker tweekers." The vibration and tones are intensified from the drug but are also compromising hearing.

Users have developed ingenious ways to conceal ecstasy tablets. They may place tablets in Pez dispensers, where the first few tablets are Pez candies and the rest are ecstasy (Pez candies may also be laced with LSD). Tootsie rolls are also softened via microwave oven and ecstasy tablets placed inside. The tootsie rolls are then rewrapped and carried into dance clubs. The use of tootsie rolls as concealment is possibly where the term "rolling on ecstasy" comes from. Skittles, mints and other candies are also used to conceal ecstasy tablets. By cutting open the package, tablets are placed inside and mixed with the candies. The packages are then resealed thwarting securities' efforts to locate contraband *(photo 7.10)*.

The company Dance Safe offers products that allow ecstasy users to test their pills to confirm they have, in fact, purchased ecstasy. The chemical testing is not precise and cannot determine if other drugs have been mixed with the ecstasy. If the tablet is not ecstasy, the testing procedure does not have the ability to confirm what the specific drug is and cannot determine the dosage of the pills *(photo 7.11)*.

Ecstasy can cause severe dehydration, elevated body temperature, rapid pulse, elevated blood pressure, and dilated pupils. It also causes relaxed inhibitions and feelings of empathy. As a user's body temperature is elevated and they engage in excessive dancing, which is common, it causes the user to become very thirsty. Promoters may turn off the water in bathrooms or water fountains and sell bottled water at inflated prices. Users consume copious amounts of water that can lead to a condition known as hyponatremia, or water toxicity. When the human body consumes large quantities of water, it disrupts the chemical balances within our bodies and the brain may begin to swell. This can lead to seizures, brain damage, and even death. Promoters may also offer cooling or misting rooms that mist water into the air to assist in cooling an individual's body temperature.

A large amount of ecstasy being marketed today actually contains no ecstasy, rather it contains drugs like ketamine, methamphetamine, LSD *(photo 7.12a, 7.12b)*, PMA, MDA *(photo 7.13)*, and a long list of others. When ecstasy is purchased at a rave, the buyer generally does not know the person selling the ecstasy and most likely may have just met them at the party. The individual may believe they purchased ecstasy but may have, in fact, purchased something even more deadly.

PMA, for example, has been sold as ecstasy but is much more powerful, and the timeline for feeling the effects is much slower. Many times the PMA pills have a Mitsubishi logo imprinted on them and are sometimes larger in thickness than ecstasy pills. Several deaths have occurred in Chicago and Florida where kids thought they were taking ecstasy and were ingesting PMA. Since the timeline for PMA is approximately three hours before the effects are felt, many kids, believing the drug was ecstasy, took a pill and waited a short time. Because they didn't feel any effects, a second and then a third pill were consumed. Once the drug began to take affect, the body temperatures became so elevated that death occurred. Body temperatures of 114 degrees have been recorded.

Ecstasy can also cause comparable body temperatures, but PMA is simply more dangerous.

The following is a list of some designer drugs that are chemically related to ecstasy but may have different effects. 5-MeO-DiPT or "Foxy" is an unpleasant hallucinogenic drug which can last up to fourteen hours. Alpha-Methyltryptamine or AMT is an amphetamine with ecstasy-like effects. 4-MTA, also known as "Flat Liners," is also a stimulant/hallucinogenic drug that gives ecstasy-like effects for about twelve hours. 4-Bromo-2,5-dimethoxyamphetamine also known as "Bromo," DOB, and STP, is 33 times more potent than ecstasy and can last for approximately eighteen hours. 2C-B or "Nexus" has a higher serotonin release than ecstasy and is generally used for its sexual stimulation with the timeline being approximately two to eight hours. Yaba means "crazy medicine" in Thailand, where it was first manufactured. It was seen as a type of super ecstasy, as it contains methamphetamine and caffeine.

I mention each one of these drugs to make you aware of how many different types of manufactured drugs are available, however, these are only a few of a continually growing list. There are approximately 200 phenethylamines and tryptamines, with ecstasy (phenethylamines) being the most well known of these two categories. We may never see any of these drugs, as they may never become popular in our area, but again, it is important to understand the terminology and be able to recognize various names of designer drugs. Remember, calling a Poison Control Center may not be able to assist you in identifying these types of pills, as they are neither prescription nor over-the-counter medication. Poison control centers are gradually becoming more aware of the effects of these drugs but the actual testing of a pill may be necessary. The only center capable of determining what the pill contains is a law enforcement crime lab.

Drugs that are legal are often sold as a look-a-like drug. Here are a few examples: Remifemin menopause tablets have a butterfly logo imprinted into them and are often sold as ecstasy *(photo 7.14)*. They are a rip-off, as no high is achieved. Excedrin aspirin tablets are imprinted with a large "E" and are also sold as ecstasy. Now ask yourself, why would your son or daughter have menopausal pills? Or why would Excedrin tablets be placed in plastic baggies rather than in the proper bottle and may even be divided into one tablet per bag? These behaviors are sending up red flags. Please don't be fooled by excuses children give and don't be satisfied with their reasons.

Finally, lysergic acid diethylamide, otherwise known as LSD, is a schedule 1 drug, which means it has no medical use nor is it legal in the United States. Ever wonder why the Salem witch trials occurred? A form of LSD, known as the ergot root, was being used probably without knowledge of its effects. The fungus found on the ergot root was brewed in teas back in the seventeenth century. This probably caused the user to hallucinate, thus setting the stage for individuals who were seen as being possessed by evil spirits.

Today the majority of LSD is produced in clandestine laboratories. In fact, the DEA believes that approximately seven pounds of LSD is produced each year for sale in the United States. Seven pounds sounds like a very small amount compared to the thousands of pounds of marijuana and cocaine that are consumed in the United States each year; however, one pound of pure LSD would be enough to dose about nine million people. Another way to visualize this would be to look at an Altoid breath tablet—if it were pure LSD it would be enough to dose about 22,000 persons. Doses of LSD are measured in micrograms, and usually containing less than 80 micrograms per dose, and are commonly sold on blotter paper and then ingested. Blotter paper is paper which is perforated into squares approximately ¼ inch by ¼ inch and may have designs of cartoon characters imprinted on it. The process of placing LSD on paper varies, but the most common way is to have sheets of blotter paper that are then dipped into trays containing liquid LSD. The blotter paper is then hung out to dry, much like laundry. Gravity pulls the LSD to the bottom of the paper that then contains larger amounts of LSD. The individual purchasing the blotter paper is unaware if there is a large or small amount of LSD contained within the paper *(photo 7.15a, 7.15b, 7.15c).*

Since LSD can also be a liquid, it can be placed in Visine or other brands of eye drop bottles or food coloring containers and then ingested by dropping the liquid into the eye or mouth. Liquid LSD is also placed onto sugar cubes, where it is then ingested orally. It can also be mixed with Knox gelatin and spread to dry and then is cut into cubes that are about a ¼ inch by ¼ inch and are commonly referred to as "window panes." Since LSD is light sensitive and it breaks down when exposed to light, it may be stored in film canisters, tin foil, wallets or any container where it is protected from light.

LSD effects are unpredictable and can depend on the amount taken, the mood a person is in during the time of ingestion, and the surroundings the person is in. As an example, loud music, mood lights, and the temperature of the room can affect LSD's effect on the brain. Besides hallucinations, users may experience a phenomenon know as "synesthesia," where sights are transposed into odors, or sounds may be transposed into sights. Here is an example: a friend of mine was conducting a DRE evaluation on a 20-year-old male and while in the police department, the telephone rang and the subject said, "Wow, do that again, do it again." As the phone rang again the subject said, "Wow, check it out, check it out!" When the officer asked what he was talking about, he said, "The rainbow, the rainbow, look at the rainbow." The sound of the telephone was transposed into the sight of a rainbow.

Red Flags for Parents (Raves)

Paraphernalia chosen by ravers is generally child oriented, including pacifiers to help control teeth grinding; Vicks VaporRub, nasal inhalers; surgical, carpenter, and gas masks; glow sticks; mouth guards; spinning toy lights; laser lights; gardening gloves; plush gloves; and vibrating massagers. Colored beaded necklaces may also be given out—usually for each ecstasy tablet purchased. High energy drinks and bottled water are again common among users. All these items aid in sensory perception as the drugs ingested will intensify ones senses (*photo 7.16*).

Kids take the time to conceal ecstasy tablets in a variety of ways, including placing tablets in with Skittles, M&M's, and other candies. Tablets are also placed on candy necklaces in between pieces of candy. Pez dispensers are also used; while the first few rows contain Pez candies, the rest of the container holds ecstasy. Another method is to microwave a Tootsie Roll to soften it and then press an ecstasy tablet inside, concealing it. The Tootsie Rolls and any candies with packaging are resealed and carried into the rave thwarting securities' efforts to locate contraband.

Disney, Sesame Street, Teletubbies, and generally any characters associated with children's cartoons are chosen by ravers to advertise clandestinely their feelings about drug use. The characters will have subtle changes like very large pupils, red eyes, or they may be holding pacifiers. So how can you tell if your child just happens to like a character? Look for T-shirts displaying the letter E or a backwards e, indicating the promoting or advertising of ecstasy. The backwards E refers to "flipping" or combining the drug ecstasy with other drugs. The term PLUR, which stands for "Peace

Love Unity Respect," may be seen on clothing or bumper stickers. Pixie fairies, fairies, or butterflies can also indicate the support of ecstasy—this includes the wearing of butterfly or angel wings on a person's back. Clothing made by numerous companies contains hidden pockets used for the concealment of various substances.

Remember, we need to look at the big picture. Don't forget that one item by itself can mean nothing; you must look at the totality of the circumstances. Changes in your child's behavior, appearance, mood, clothing, and friends can be indicative of warning signs. Know where your child is going and don't be afraid to investigate.

Another red flag would be locating any books written by Alexander Shulgin otherwise known as "Sasha" or "Papa Ecstasy." Shulgin has claimed to have developed and/or self-tested hundreds of psychoactive chemicals. His books include *The Simple Plant Isoquinolines*, which describes the chemical structure of plants and their effects, *Controlled Substances: Chemicals & Legal Guide to Federal Drug Laws* and finally the books *TiHKAL* and *PiHKAL*. *TiHKAL* stands for *Tryptamines i Have Known And Loved: The Continuation"* and *PiHKAL* which stands for *Phenethylamines i Have Known and Loved: A Chemical Love Story"* and contributed a chapter to *Entheogens and the Future of Religion*. Each one of these books describes designer drugs or drugs that have been developed by man for either hallucinogenic or sensory type experiences.

Red Flags for Parents (LSD)

I have found LSD blotter paper wrapped in cellophane, tin foil, and hidden in wallets, film canisters, and Game Boy cartridges. Keep this in mind when searching—LSD blotter paper is so small it is easy to hide but must be stored away from direct light. This, again, is because the chemical LSD will break down when exposed to light. LSD may also be dropped on sugar cubes or hidden in food coloring bottles or other small bottles. Once again, these items will generally be kept away from light sources.

Identifying Pills

Ecstasy tablets can have numerous colors, shapes, and design logos. The Drug Enforcement Administration has noted over 600 different pill insignias. The pills generally have logos or imprints on them much like prescription medications have some type of identifying marks. Ecstasy logos may have the arches from the McDonald's symbol, dolphins, doves, Playboy bunnies, smiley faces, king's crowns, horses…the list is endless. We just need to look at the pill and observe that the markings are inconsistent with that of medical pills.

Finding the pills can also be a challenge. As we talked about in Chapter 2, it is easy to hide or camouflage drugs. Because ecstasy is a pill it can be easily mixed in with other pills. Simply placing the ecstasy tablets in a bottle containing Tylenol, Excedrin, aspirin, prescription medications or candies can make it difficult to locate these pills. We need to open up containers to see if the pill designs all match. The only way to determine if a pill is, in fact, ecstasy is for chemical testing from a law enforcement crime lab.

Physical Signs Associated with Hallucinogens

The following are signs and symptoms associated with hallucinogenic drugs: elevated body temperature, pulse, and blood pressure; hallucinations; synesthesia; dazed appearance; body tremors; paranoia; perspiration; disorientation; nausea; goose bumps; statements suggesting hallucinations; difficulty in swallowing and speaking; light sensitivity; confusion; combative behaviors; and flashbacks. Individuals may be irritable for several days after a weekend party because of the depletion of serotonin and dopamine.

Common Terms Used by Ravers

E-Tard:	A spin off of "retard," which refers to a chronic ecstasy user
Rolling:	Being high or tripping on ecstasy
E-Puddle:	A group of kids rubbing and touching each other
Peeps:	Nickname given to the dilation of the pupils caused by ecstasy
Plug Faces:	Refers to using pacifiers because of the teeth grinding
Piggybacking:	Refers to taking several ecstasy tablets throughout the night
PLUR:	Peace Love Unity Respect

Street Terminology

Mushrooms	Ecstasy	LSD	Peyote
Shrooms	Adam	Acid	Cactus
Buttons	E	Window Panes	Buttons
Caps	Love Drug	Tabs	Chief
Magic Mushrooms	Hug Drug	Blotter Acid	Dry Whisky
Psilocybin	Batman	Microdots	Topi
Spores	Rolling	Paper Acid	Tops
Funny Shrooms	XTC	Blotter	Mesc
Sacred Shrooms	Eve	Cube	Mescal
Blue Halo	Scooby Snacks	Dot	Mescaline
Teonanacati	Debs	Big D	Mescalito
Food of the Gods	Charity	Blue Heaven	Peyoti
Boomers	Cristal	Sheet	
Musk	Wheels	L	
Silly Putty	Iboga	Sandoz	
Simple Simon	Dex	Sid	
	X	California Sunshine	

CHAPTER 8

Dissociative Anesthetics

PCP was originally developed in the 1950s as a dissociative anesthetic intended for surgery, but when patients came out of surgery, a large majority had delusions, hallucinations and psychotic behaviors, some of which were permanent. Because of these issues it was discontinued for use in human surgery, but was utilized in veterinarian surgery, until it was dropped for all use.

In 1978 PCP became a Scheduled 1 Drug in the Controlled Substance Act and is no longer produced for medical purposes; however, it is still produced in clandestine laboratories. PCP is mostly seen in large cities but has also been found in smaller communities. Depending on the manufacturing process, PCP can have a chemical odor or no odor at all. The color can vary from white to brown for powder, and liquid can look like apple juice. There are hundreds of chemical analogs or chemical cousins to PCP, such as PCE and TCP. As stated earlier, an analog is a drug that is chemically related to another drug. It is like going to the doctor with a cold and getting a prescription for penicillin; if the penicillin doesn't work, you might then get a prescription for amoxicillin. The two drugs are chemically related but have some different effects. Drugs like ketamine, tiletamine, Ketalar, Ketaset and numerous others were developed to replace PCP, seeking drugs with fewer side effects. Some were made for human and pediatric use, while others were used as animal tranquilizers.

PCP has some of the effects from each of the last three categories we talked about. It can be like a depressant, stimulant, or hallucinogen. As a depressant, a person could exhibit drunk-like behaviors, loss of coordination, and nausea. The stimulant effects exhibited are elevated pulse and blood pressure, along with elevated body temperature, dry mouth, and muscle rigidity. Finally, like a hallucinogen, PCP can cause hallucinations, paranoia, and delusions. The effects of PCP are like flipping a coin, because you never know what behaviors to expect. It is unknown what causes the wide range of behaviors in individuals—from violent to calm to cyclic mood swings. Like most drugs, PCP and its analogs are body weight-dose equivalent, and the effects vary depending on the amount ingested, its purity level, and if it is mixed with any other drugs. There is no quality control in the manufacturing process of PCP, as each method of cooking can produce varying levels of purity. Therefore, an individual can try a drug just once and have seizures, lapse into a coma, or have a fatal reaction.

Because PCP was developed as a dissociative anesthetic, it causes the user to have loss of sensitivity to pain. This is where the legendary stories of superhuman strength are derived from. There are no documented stories of actual increased strength; however, stories abound regarding individuals unaffected by pain, who continue their bizarre behavior despite broken bones, gunshot wounds, et cetera, that would stop a normal person. Police cases across the country have been televised where an officer's use of force was questionable. When I see these events unfold, I am always curious to see what the toxicology results of the suspect are and to see if PCP or one of its analogs was listed as a drug. Knowing that a person under the effects of PCP can feel no pain can give a better understanding of an officer's actions when dealing with these individuals in certain situations.

In 1991 the infamous Los Angeles police incident where Rodney King was "beaten" caused riots and disturbances across the country, yet his toxicological results indicated the presence of PCP. In Ohio in 2003, an African American male, Nathaniel Jones, was also "beaten" by police during an altercation after a traffic stop. Again, PCP and also cocaine were detected in his system. These remarks are not intended to justify police actions. They are intended to provide information on how difficult dealing with someone under the influence of PCP can be.

Methods of Ingestion

The common methods of ingesting PCP are to snort, swallow or to smoke it. The effects of the drug begin within one to five minutes after ingestion and last approximately four to six hours. Powdered and liquid PCP is often mixed with tobacco cigarettes, marijuana cigarettes, or mixed with parsley, sage, mint and various other spices. Some users do this to kill the taste of the chemicals, while others say the mint and other spices have a cooling sensation. All of these products can also be dipped into liquid PCP, which is difficult to recognize. Depending on the type of product being smoked, you may be able to see discoloration on the paper; however, the best way is to smell the item and determine if it has a chemical odor.

Sherm cigarettes are also used, because they are brown in color and will not be discolored by the liquid PCP. Liquid PCP can also be poured into Visine bottles and then dropped into the eye as another form of ingestion. Very little of the drug is actually absorbed through the eye because much of it runs out and down the cheek. A smaller portion of the drug may enter into the tear duct and into the sinus passages where it is absorbed into the body.

Wet sticks known as "wets," "fries," "frys," or "illies" are tobacco or marijuana cigarettes soaked in embalming fluid, ether, or liquid PCP. This is extremely dangerous, as embalming fluid contains toxins like formaldehyde and methanol that can cause death. Embalming fluid was mixed with PCP in years past as a means of slowing the burn of the cigarette, resulting in a nickname for PCP of "embalming fluid." In more recent years, abusers have misunderstood and began deliberately abusing actual embalming fluid by itself. Bizarre behavior does result from this practice, though it does not give the same pain block effect as PCP.

The effect of PCP generally lasts four to six hours and depends on the manufacturing process and purity level. As PCP is eliminated from our bodies, some can be stored in the fat cells. Generally, when a hallucinogenic drug is ingested, a person can have a flashback or a memory of the "trip" they previously experienced when ingesting the drug, somewhat like a day dream. PCP, on the other hand, can be stored in the body's cells and released into the body several months after ingestion at any time without warning.

Ketamine

Ketamine was developed in the 1960s and is being abused by kids today. Ketamine, Telazol and others are similar to PCP in some respects. Ketamine is an animal tranquilizer used in veterinary surgeries across the country and used in some pediatric procedures *(photo 8.1)*. It is also a "battlefield" anesthetic. How do kids obtain ketamine? They simply burglarize area veterinarian clinics overlooking cash and stealing the ketamine, or they order it over the internet. Or if you live near the Mexican border, an easy way to obtain ketamine is to cross the border and purchase ketamine at a Mexican pharmacy, where the drug laws are less strict. Once the bottles are purchased, individuals smuggle them into the United States. On the street a bottle of liquid ketamine can be worth in excess of $200.

So why and how is the ketamine converted into a powder? Liquid ketamine is generally not injected, because it acts as a powerful tranquilizer rapidly incapacitating an individual. That is why liquid ketamine is converted into a powder or simply added to a drink. Placing the liquid into an oven or microwave at low temperatures will cause the ketamine to crystallize, which can then be smoked or snorted. The ketamine powder can also be placed into tobacco products or marijuana cigarettes, or it can be cut into lines and snorted, much like cocaine. Doses of ketamine or PCP are known on the streets as "bumps" and usually contain 1/20 of a gram.

Drug users or individuals experimenting with drugs do not want to become catatonic. The desired effect is to consume just enough of the drug to obtain euphoria. Ketamine is also a preferred drug of the rave culture for its hallucinogenic effects. Ketamine in low doses can produce a mellow, dreamy feeling known as "K-land." In high doses ketamine can produce distorted perceptions of both auditory and visual senses, even unconsciousness can occur. This type of experience is referred to as a "K-hole," which is the threshold many users are looking for. Ketamine users may be in designated corners at raves as they are experiencing hallucinogenic effects of the drug. Their movements may be very slow and deliberate and they could have difficulty walking; they may be unable to move at all, making them open to assault. Since ketamine is closely related to PCP, violent behavior is rare, but possible.

Again, depending on the dose, ketamine can act like an anesthetic, also producing amnesia. This is not preferred by individuals attempting to get high, but is preferred by those committing sexual assaults. For this reason ketamine is also known as a date rape drug, metabolizing very rapidly in the body and is usually eliminated within approximately 48 hours.

Methods of Ingestion of Ketamine

Ketamine is commercially manufactured as a powder or liquid; however, obtaining the powder is more difficult than obtaining the liquid. As discussed previously, it does not take much effort to convert the liquid to powder where it can then be snorted, injected or smoked. As with most drugs, users develop a tolerance and require more of the drug to obtain the same high. Its effects can be addictive.

Red Flags for Parents

One of the main ingredients in the production of PCP is the chemical piperdine, which is difficult to obtain as it is controlled by federal law. Pyrrolidine, another chemical which is easier to obtain, can be substituted for piperdine by individuals making PCP. Locating bottles of piperdine or pyrrolidine are huge red flags for parents. Look for glass vials hidden in bedrooms, which contain a strong chemical odor, or powder usually wrapped in tinfoil or plastic baggies. Take note of any glass bottles or packaging material with the words ketamine or any of its analogs or stating "research chemicals."

Not everyone advertises their drug use, however, if they do, look for hats, T-shirts, and scribbling on folders with the lettering of Special K, or Special K "reshape your mind," K-hole (the rim of reality), K-mart T-shirts, "ketamine" not just for cats, Circle K T-shirts, Ketamine "be as bad as you want to be," or Planet K.

Physical Signs Associated with Dissociative Anesthetics

The following are signs and symptoms associated with the use of dissociative anesthetics: elevated pulse, blood pressure, and body temperature; robotic-like movements; slowed responses; rigid muscle tone; cyclic mood swings; warm to the touch; possibly violent; perspiring heavily; impaired perception of time and distance; chemical odor; agitated; paranoid; blank stare; nonresponsive; respiratory depression; memory loss; noncommunicative; amnesia; disoriented; delusions; out-of-body sensations; hallucinations; numbness; nausea; vomiting; slurred responses; stepping over inanimate objects.

Street Terminology			
PCP		**Ketamine**	
PCP	Peace Pill	Special K	
Angel Dust	Devil Dust	Super K	Lady K
Peace	Ace	Vitamin K	KJ
Lovely	Paz	Green K	K
Gas	Amp	Kit Kat	Crystal
Zombie	Boat	Elephant Tranquilizer	Jet
Jet Fuel	Pinners	Horse Tranquilizer	Honey oil
Monkey	Rhino	Animal Tranquilizer	Cat Valium
Embalming Fluid	Dust	Super C	Tranq
Super Kools	Kools	Super Acid	Ket
Killer	Tic-tac	Special la Coke	Vet
Rocket Fuel	DOA		

CHAPTER 9

Narcotics

There are three categories of narcotics: naturally occurring (those derived from opium), synthetic or man-made, and semi-synthetic, which has both natural and synthetic chemicals. We generally think that narcotics are injected illegally or taken orally if legally prescribed. Not all narcotics are injected; many are snorted and even smoked.

Heroin
In the 1860s, when the United States was involved in the Civil War, the medical facilities were far from modern. Many of the men who were shot or injured died from complications. One of the drugs administered for pain was morphine and became known as the "soldiers' drug." Because it was so highly addictive, scientists developed heroin hoping it would be less addictive. Unfortunately, heroin was just as addictive as morphine, creating a new epidemic.

During the early 1900s heroin could be found in over-the-counter medicines for the treatment of insomnia and diarrhea. Heroin comes from the opium poppy, which is harvested in the Golden Crescent—Afghanistan, Pakistan, and Iran or the Golden Triangle—Burma, Laos, and Thailand. Even Mexico has become involved in the growing of heroin. Pure heroin is white in color and the shade varies depending on where it is from and its manufacturing process *(photo 9.1a, 9.1b, 9.1c)*. Just as cocaine is not always white, heroin is also not always white.

Injecting heroin is very easy. It requires a hypodermic needle, some type of tourniquet, a lighter, a spoon, a bottle cap or the bottom of a soda can, a small cotton ball (about the size of a pea) or the tip of a filtered cigarette. About one-tenth of a gram of heroin is placed on the spoon, bottle cap, or soda can along with about 20 cc of water. The bottom is then heated, and as it begins to boil, a filter (the cotton ball or cigarette tip) is placed in the spoon. This process is referred to as "cooking" and the heroin is now ready to be injected via a hypodermic needle *(photo 9.2, 9.3, 9.4, 9.5)*. The heroin is drawn into the hypodermic needle from the filter and is then set aside, allowing it to cool. The heroin can be injected either subcutaneously (under the skin), which is referred to as "skin poppin," into a vein, or into an artery called "main lining." A typical user will inject several times a day. So why do some users choose to inject in a vein, muscle, or an artery? Injecting in the vein or artery will give a very intense euphoria with a very rapid onset, while injecting into muscle tissue or subcutaneously causes a slow onset; however, the effects last longer and are not as intense.

The bottom of the spoon, soda can, or bottle cap will become discolored from cooking or heating the bottom of the item. The pea-size cotton ball also becomes discolored depending upon the color of the heroin. The cotton balls are saved and if the user does not have the money for heroin, they will soak the used cotton balls in water, extract the heroin by "cooking-up" the water/heroin mixture, and then inject it. Individuals become so addicted to the drug they will even suck on the used cotton balls to extract the last little bit of the drug *(photo 9.7)*.

To determine if a hypodermic needle is used for street drugs or medical use, look at the syringe portion to see if the inside contains trace amounts of blood. Users will inject the heroin, leave the needle in their vein, and draw their own blood back into the syringe and then reinject their own blood. This may be done several times. The reason for doing this is because trace amounts of the drug are left inside the syringe after injecting, and users do not want to waste any of the heroin. The street term for reinjecting your own blood is commonly referred to as "jacking off the needle," "flushing out the needle," or "washing." If your child says they have a syringe because their friend is diabetic and the syringe contains dried blood, I would be very concerned as diabetics don't inject into a vein.

Each user can prefer a different location for injecting for various reasons. Any method delivers caustic chemicals into the body. As the user continues to inject, they develop ulcerations, sores, and can even develop gangrene in areas where they continue to inject. Because needles are commonly shared among users, they become exposed to diseases like AIDS, hepatitis, and even tuberculosis. As sores and scabs form, users will pick-up the scab and inject underneath it, then press the scab back down covering the injection site. This is frequently referred to among users as "trap dooring" and is commonly done to hide multiple injection sites.

Users will inject anywhere—in the arms, legs, neck, between the toes, and underneath the nails. They generally attempt to hide their injection spots. Guys will paint their toe nails or finger nails, injecting under the painted nails; tattoos are also a place to hide injection spots, as the coloring makes it difficult to detect *(photo 9.8)*. One telltale sign is by looking closely at the tattoo to see if the ink has bleed or run *(photo 9.9)*. It is very unusual for tattoo ink to bleed unless drugs have been injected under the ink.

There is also the "sweet spot," which is a location users don't inject in very often unless other areas are becoming severely infected or veins are collapsing. The sweet spot may be on the underside of the tongue, the side of the eye, the penis, or the vagina. Through training I became aware of a 19-year-old male in the Baltimore area who had been injecting heroin into the vein of his penis and over time developed gangrene. This resulted in the removal of a portion of his penis.

"Cheese" is the street term for the combination of heroin, acetaminophen, and diphenhydramine and has been very popular in the Dallas, Texas, area. Cheese is prevalent among juveniles, with users snorting the powder much like snorting cocaine. The physical signs and symptoms would be like combining a narcotic and a depressant. Please refer to the sections on physical signs and symptoms in the chapters on narcotics and depressants or the upcoming chapter Combining Drugs.

As I stated earlier, drug use is not a victimless crime. We are the victims whether they are violent crimes or property crimes. The average heroin user has about a $50 a day habit. A pawn shop usually pays out 10 percent of the value of property brought in. If we have an unemployed heroin user, they must steal $500 a day worth of property to pawn in order to support a $50 a day habit. This means one heroin user is stealing approximately $182,500 a year worth of stolen property. In a city the size of New York or Los Angeles, there are thousands of heroin users. This example is regarding only one type of drug abuser; when you factor in all the other types of drug abusers, the cost to society is astronomical.

OxyContin

OxyContin contains oxycodone and is one of the most abused narcotics as it is prescribed for moderate to severe pain. Like other narcotics, it is abused for its euphoric effects. OxyContin was designed to contain a time-release mechanism, which allows the medications to be released into the body slowly throughout the day for pain management. It is available in 10, 20, 40, and 80 milligram doses and is usually imprinted with the letters "OC" on one side and may have the number of the dose on the other side *(photo 9.10)*. The cost per tablet is generally about one dollar per milligram. Users are well aware of the time-release mechanism and have discovered how to circumvent the protective coating. They simply suck off or file off the time-release coating, then crush or grind up the tablets which can then be snorted or injected. Many heroin users even prefer OxyContin over street heroin as they know what they are buying, and the effects can be more intense and last several hours longer. With street drugs, users might not know what they are purchasing.

Users know prescription drugs are pure and unadulterated, unlike street drugs, so there is no reason to cook them up. The prescription pill is simply crushed up and placed on a spoon; water is then added on top of the pill and the cotton ball is put on top. Then the hypodermic needle is placed on top of the cotton ball and the medication is drawn up through the needle. The cotton ball acts like a filter to prevent larger portions of the pill from being drawn up into the needle causing it to clog.

The Top Prescription Narcotics Being Abused

Vicodin, or hydrocodone *(photo 9.11)*, is a narcotic prescribed for moderate pain and is given often after surgery. It is highly addictive as most narcotics are. Packer's Quarterback Brett Favre fought an addiction to pain killers due to injuries he received early in his career. Drugs do not care about your professional or economic status—they can affect anyone!

If you have ever had to have surgery, remember how euphoric you felt when you returned to your room? Do you also remember asking for water or ice? And your voice was probably low and raspy. This is because narcotics dry out various systems of the body. The voice box becomes irritated from lack of lubrication causing the raspy voice. Do you remember that one of the requirements to leave the hospital was to have a bowel movement? This is because narcotics also cause constipation, because they also dry out the colon. Do you also remember itching or scratching your face or chest? This is again because of the skin drying out from the use of the narcotic. Continued use can lead to facial scabs or sores from scratching.

The following is a list of the most commonly abused narcotics and what they are normally prescribed for. Narcotic users will frequently substitute any of these drugs to prevent them from going through withdrawal.

Dilaudid, or hydromorphone, is prescribed for moderate to severe pain and is given to burn victims and cancer patients.

Demerol is usually given to patients after surgery for moderate to severe pain; unlike most narcotics, Demerol may not cause a constriction of the pupils but may actually dilate them.

MS Cotin is morphine sulfate *(photo 9.12)* and is a controlled-release drug that can last up to twelve hours. Crushing or chewing this drug breaks down the time-release mechanism and can release a dangerous amount of morphine into the body at one time that can even lead to death. OxyContin users often substitute this drug for OxyContin.

Percocet, which is oxycodone hydrochloride and contains acetaminophen, is used to control moderate to severe pain.

Roxicet contains oxycodone and Tylenol and are prescribed for moderate to severe pain. The abuse level is extremely high.

Morphine patches are placed onto the skin and are absorbed directly into the body. Abusers may place multiple patches on various portions of their bodies or may extract the morphine from the patch where it can then be injected or smoked.

Fentanyl, known as Duragesic, is another drug that can be prescribed as a patch. The patch is placed on the body much like a bandage and is designed to continually release a dose of the pain killer into the body, where other narcotics had failed to give relief *(photo 9.13, 9.14)*. The fentanyl is then absorbed into the body through the skin, just like the morphine patch. Unfortunately, the fentanyl patch looks a lot like a morphine patch. Fentanyl is about one hundred times more powerful than morphine, and morphine is about ten times more powerful than heroin. Because fentanyl is such a potent drug many individuals, who have extracted the fentanyl from the patch in an attempt to inject it, have met with an untimely death. Methods of ingestion vary, but users have been known to freeze the patches and suck on them, or place the patch on the skin and use a hair dryer to apply heat to the patch to increase how fast the drug enters the body. Some individuals have even used the patch as a suppository, where the drug is quickly absorbed into the colon.

Methadone is commonly given to heroin users to wean them off of the heroin in hopes they will no longer be addicted. However, keep in mind that methadone tablets are also prescribed to individuals for pain management.

One of the newest things on the market is **Actiq** *(see photo 9.14)*, a sucker that contains fentanyl citrate, which is given to persons in chronic pain. These drugs were developed to help cancer patients relieve pain. Actiq suckers can be sucked on or licked distributing the drug into the body. The Actiq sucker on the street is known as a perco-pop and can contain 200–1600 milligrams of fentanyl and sells anywhere from $20–$40.

Stadol NS is a nasal spray in a narcotic form and is highly addictive. A 2 milligram dose of Stadol is equal to 10 milligrams of morphine, 40 milligrams of Talwin Nx, or 80 milligrams of Demerol.

Codeine is found in numerous cold medications and sometimes combined with Guaifenesin which is a cough expectorant with stimulant properties *(photo 9.15)*.

These are just a general list of common prescription narcotics. Remember, drugs within this category affect the body in the same manner. Again, if you locate pills and are unsure what they may be, call the Poison Control Center at 1-800-222-1222 , or use local pharmacies, hospitals, or WebMD@ www.webmd.com. Once you determine the type of pill or pills, the physical effect your child exhibited or is exhibiting can confirm your suspicions. Remember, if drugs are ingested, medical intervention is probably necessary.

Methods of Ingestion

The methods of ingestion for narcotics vary depending on the type of substance used and what method the user prefers. Many users prefer injecting the drug because of the intense "rush" they feel. Again, like stimulant users, needles are shared and the spread of disease is common. Track marks will occur after continued injections leaving sores and infection *(photo 9.16a, 9.16b, 9.16c)*. Users will also inject via "trap dooring," which is picking up a scab or sore and injecting underneath it. This hides the new injection site making it more difficult to observe. Tattoos are a common place to hide injection sites. Also remember the "sweet spot," an area users only inject in occasionally and may include the penis, vagina, eyes, underneath the tongue or other difficult areas to examine.

Narcotics may also be smoked or snorted causing many of the same problems as the stimulant users who choose to ingest drugs in the same fashion. Like snorting cocaine, narcotics will also cause a deterioration of the septum leading to a hole between the nostrils, along with infections and other sinus problems.

If narcotic patches, such as morphine and fentanyl, are the desired type of drug, they are generally placed on the body under clothing where they are covertly hidden *(photo 9.17)*. The drug then absorbs into the body over the course of a few hours. Patches may also be sucked on and even placed inside the rectum or vagina for absorption into the body.

Many prescription narcotics are taken orally, by enema, or placed inside the anus for absorption.

⚑ Red Flags for Parents

As stated previously in this book, the first thing to notice would be the pupils. The narcotic user's pupils will constrict to about the size of a pinpoint *(photo 9.18a, 9.18b)*. No other drug will affect the eyes in this manner.

Be observant of individuals with a dry mouth, continually licking the inside of their mouth or asking for water. The dry mouth will also lead to a raspy voice. Individuals may purchase ex-lax or some type of laxative to assist them in going to the bathroom.

Also be aware of track marks or ulcerations on the skin from injecting via hypodermic needles. If a person is injecting, look for long sleeve shirts being worn all year long to hide track marks. Also look for hypodermic needles with dried blood in the syringe, a tourniquet-type of device with possible traces of blood, cotton balls or Q-tips where the cotton is torn off and rolled to about the size of a pea, or the tip of a cigarette filter. These are used to filter impurities from street drugs. Look for burn marks on the bottom of spoons, bottle caps, or the bottom side of a soda can. These items are used to heat up or cook illegal drugs *(photo 9.19)*.

Cotton and cigarette filters are also used in the injection of prescription medication. Prescription meds do not have to be cooked to remove impurities; however, they are still filtered, because many of the binders contained within the pill can clog the hypodermic needle.

Remember to check all pill bottles, even if they say a brand name like Tylenol or Excedrin. Prescription pills are often mixed in with other pills in legitimate containers.

Heroin is often packaged for personal use in small balloons which have been tied off. Also used are small plastic dime baggies that generally have some type of printed label, like dice or cartoon characters, which is usually the dealer's logo. Heroin can also be hidden in cellophane, gum wrappers, or tinfoil that has been folded up into very small squares containing about one-tenth of a gram of heroin

Physical Signs Associated with Narcotic Use

The following is a list of the signs and symptoms associated with narcotic use: body temperature is lowered along with pulse, blood pressure, and respiration; facial and body itching; nausea; vomiting; constipation; low raspy voice and a dry mouth; sleepy appearance; droopy eyelids; track marks; injection sites; fresh puncture marks; skin irritation *(photo 9.20)*; semiconscious state; sedation; large consumption of soda or water after use; gum line of the mouth becomes ulcerated and develops the soft-like consistency of a banana.

Street Terminology		Prescription
Heroin		**Prescription**
Junk	Brown	OxyContin
Balloons	Big Daddy	Oxy
Spoon	Brown Sugar	Hillbilly Heroin
Horse	Hombre	Caucasian Cocaine
Smack	Stoffa	Midwest Heroin
Downtown	Gum	Poorman's Heroin
School Boy	Gumball	Prescription Heroin
Chiva	Gomero	O's
Chasing the Dragon	Chocolate	Oceans
Stuff	Mexican Mud	Ox
Boy	Pedazo	Patches
China White	Tootsie Roll	40s
Dope	Smeck	80s
Tar	Black Tar	Kicker
Buggers	Rufus	
Shit	Scag	
Goma	Dyno	
P-funk	Big H	
His	Antifreeze	
H	Harry	

CHAPTER 10

Inhalants

Inhalants are broken down into four categories: volatile solvents, aerosols, anesthetic gases, and nitrates. Volatile solvents refer to gasoline, glues, paint thinners, and hundreds of other chemicals. Aerosols are chemicals contained under pressurized cans—examples are Glade, Pam, Dust-Off, hair sprays, and numerous others. Anesthetic gases refer to nitrous oxide. Nitrates are different from other inhalants, because their primary use is sexual enhancement.

Any of these substances are ingested in several ways. The first method is directly from the source; an example is simply opening a jar of Wite-Out or a Magic Marker and holding it underneath your nose to smell the vapors. The second method is referred to as "huffing." An individual sprays the contents into a plastic bag and then places the bag over the nose and mouth and breathes the fumes. In some cases, the bag is placed over a person's head and tied around their neck, and when the person feels light-headed, the bag is removed. Unfortunately, many kids have died, unable to regain consciousness after they deprive their body of oxygen. Another way is by saturating a cloth with a chemical and placing it over your nose and mouth and inhaling the vapors *(photo 10.1, 10.2, 10.3)*. Some users also place the saturated rag directly into their mouth or into a plastic bag and then inhale the fumes. Placing the cloth into the bag simply allows less of the vapors to escape and keeps the fumes concentrated in the fabric.

While traveling on Interstate 94 in the Chicago area, I observed a motor vehicle operator continually spraying the contents of an aerosol can directly onto his clothing. The windows of his vehicle were closed, allowing him to inhale the fumes while driving. One of the most bizarre methods is to spray an aerosol directly into the sinuses via the nose. Many states do not even have laws regarding the use of inhalants, and many adults and kids are well aware of that fact. However, most states do have laws that make it a crime to abuse inhalants while operating a vehicle.

There are thousands of inhalants being abused *(photo 10.4)*. Do not minimize a child abusing inhalants by thinking of it as just a passing fad, as inhalants are dangerous and can be deadly. Because inhalants deprive the brain of oxygen, continued use can lead to brain damage, neurological disorders, and in some cases, even death. Inhalant abuse can cause Sudden Sniffing Death Syndrome (SSDS), which reduces the ability of the body to carry oxygen to various parts of the body, including the brain. This can lead to blackouts, brain damage, and death. The immune system is also compromised, leading to increased infections, cirrhosis of the liver, increased risk of leukemia, and reproductive complications. Burn injuries are also prevalent for users of flammable inhalants.

All inhalants are very fast acting and, depending on how much is consumed, exit the body rapidly. As the chemical substance is taken away, our body tries to immediately eliminate the solvent as we begin breathing fresh oxygen. In fact, law enforcement laboratories usually have only a 10 percent chance of obtaining a positive test for a person who just abused inhalants. Inhalant abuse is more prevalent among males than females, and part of the reason that many kids choose inhalants over other drugs is that they are inexpensive and legal to purchase.

Volatile Solvents

Volatile solvents are liquids that include gasoline, airplane glue, dry cleaning fluids, nail polish remover, Wite-Out, felt-tip markers, and countless others. Many of these products contain chemicals such as toluene, benzene, acetone, and numerous others that were not intended to be ingested into the body. The liquids vaporize at room temperature and are inhaled in the variety of methods we read about above. When volatile solvents are inhaled in confined spaces, additional concerns arise because of how flammable they are.

Nitrous Oxide

Nitrous oxide is commonly referred to as laughing gas and is contained in several different products. Nitrous oxide is contained in large cylinders for use at dentists' offices or for medical procedures at hospitals for anesthetic effects. The cylinders are often stolen and sold to individuals, who, in turn, sell balloons filled with nitrous oxide at large parties or concerts. There are also automobile performance products that contain nitrous oxide. Many performance companies are aware of the abuse of nitrous oxide by kids and most have added sulfur to the nitrous oxide to prevent abuse.

There are also small cylinders of nitrous oxide used by restaurants and coffee houses for making whipped cream. On the street, kids refer to these cylinders as "whip-its." Nitrous oxide is pressurized and cannot be directly ingested from the source due to its extremely cold nature. If a person were to ingest it from the source, extreme lung damage, including frost bite, could occur. A product known as a "cracker" was developed and is used in conjunction with a nitrous oxide cylinder *(photo 10.5)*.

The nitrous oxide cylinder is placed in the cracker which is then screwed together *(photo 10.6a, 10.6b)*. A pin inside the cracker breaks the seal of the nitrous oxide and dispenses the contents into a balloon, which is attached to the cracker *(photo 10.6c)*. The balloon warms the nitrous oxide to room temperature, where it can then be inhaled. Typically abusers will use punching bag-type balloons, which can withstand the rapid inflation and initial cold temperature *(photo 10.6d)*.

Reddi-wip also uses nitrous oxide as a propellant to expel the whipped cream and helps to make the cream frothy *(photo 10.7)*. To use the whipped cream canister on food products, we simply tilt the can down, press on the tip and dispense the cream. Kids who are ingesting the nitrous oxide from the Reddi-wip can hold it upright, place a balloon on the tip, then press on the tip, rather than dispensing the whipped cream, the nitrous oxide is dispensed into the balloon where it is then inhaled *(photo 10.8a, 10.8b)*. Finding punching bag balloons with Reddi-wip cans are huge red flags for parents.

Aerosols

Aerosols are sprays that are propelled from cans and contain various solvents. What makes one inhalant preferred over another is generally based on the users' prior experience with the chemical or the taste. Spray paints, Pam Cooking Spray, Glad aerosols, spray-on deodorants and fabric protectors, and most recently Dust-Off, are all commonly abused inhalants. The list is endless and kids experiment with different types of products trying to find those that taste better and give longer lasting highs. Pam Cooking Spray also has a preferred taste to it, however, it is especially deadly, as over time it coats a person's lungs much like it does a pan. Eventually, as a person breathes in fresh air and it enters into the lungs, the oxygen is unable to pass into the bloodstream and the user can suffocate.

Gold and silver spray paint is generally preferred over other paints because users say it has a fruity taste to it and contains higher levels of toluene. However, any color of spray paint can be abused; it is usually personal preference or what was available.

Nitrates

Nitrates include cyclohexyl, amyl, and butyl nitrates. Of the nitrates, amyl nitrates are the most popular and are legally prescribed for individuals with heart pain. Ampoules of amyl nitrates are stolen or diverted to be sold on the streets. The terms "poppers" and "snappers" refer to amyl nitrates as the ampoule is broken and then inhaled. The nitrates are sexual enhancers and stimulate vasodilatation, which can cause an erection for extended periods of time, and is being abused in both the hetero and homosexual communities. Some individuals even combine Viagra with nitrates; however warnings have been given by the manufacturer of Viagra about the hazards of combining drugs. Many nitrates are purchased at adult book stores and head shops and are marketed as video head cleaners. Common product names are Rush, Ram, Liquid Gold, Quicksilver, Rock Hard, and video head cleaner.

Oxygen Bars

One of the newest fads in recreational entertainment is inhaling pure oxygen. Believe it or not, there are even oxygen bars where individuals inhale pure oxygen; people can even purchase cans of oxygen to inhale for the purpose of increasing energy. There is no proven research that inhaling oxygen will provide an increase in energy nor has any research been conducted on the long term effects of inhaling oxygen. Medical personnel believe that individuals with medical conditions could be affected negatively from inhaling extra oxygen. People with asthma, emphysema, and other pulmonary conditions can have adverse reaction to too much oxygen. Our bodies were designed to breathe oxygen, but not large amounts over extended periods of time. It is too early to determine what the exact effects will be from inhaling too much oxygen, but as with most legal substances, there are recommended doses, and oxygen bars go well beyond what the norm would be.

Red Flags for Parents

Be aware of empty spray paint cans, especially gold and silver, and any household chemical products hidden in bedrooms or vehicles. Examples are Glade aerosols, Pam Cooking Spray, model airplane glue, mineral spirits, Dust-Off, or any chemical products along with plastic bags containing rags with a strong chemical odor. Be cognizant of chemical odors coming from your child's clothing or their bedroom, where many kids prefer to use inhalants. It is common for kids to think the smells of household chemicals can be easily explained away. Does your child normally clean their room, or is it more of a punishment?

Vehicles are also common places to use inhalants, and there are numerous cases of kids huffing inhalants in a vehicle, then lighting up a cigarette and an explosion occurs from all of the fumes. Many kids have been severely injured during these incidents. Keep in mind, a strong chemical odor coming from the interior of a vehicle can mean inhalant abuse.

A common practice by inhalant users is to spray a substance into an empty soda can or bottle, then place it up to their mouth and inhale. It appears the person is drinking a soda but is actually inhaling the vapors of a chemical. The inside of the soda can will have a pungent chemical odor. Also look for paint residue on the hands or face. Check long-sleeve shirts for residue of paints or chemical odors on the cuffs of the sleeves. Abusers often soak the cuff in a chemical, and sit in school with their hand on their cheek and the cuff of the sleeve next to their nose. They are then able to inhale the substance in class directly in front of the teacher.

Most kids now have CD players or i-Pods. Very few have or use video tape players or audio cassette players anymore. When you are searching their room look for video head cleaner, which is a commonly abused inhalant. Ask yourself this—if your child does not have a video or audio tape player in their room, why would they have the cleaner? It is most likely because they are abusing the chemical and are very likely to be sexually active, as video head cleaners contain amyl nitrates, which are used as sexual enhancers.

If nitrous oxide is suspected, look for empty cans of Reddi-wip or nitrous oxide cylinders, along with large punching bag-type balloons and a cracker. Also look for stacked Starbucks coffee cups, as kids who work there have been known to place a nitrous oxide container in a cup, then place another cup inside the first one. The top cup will contain coffee and can easily be taken out of the store. If you find two Starbucks coffee cups stacked together and there is no coffee stain in the bottom of either cup it should cause suspicion.

Physical Signs Associated with Inhalants

The signs and symptoms that become evident when inhaling various chemicals are much like someone who is under the influence of alcohol—their face becomes flushed; they may have bloodshot, glassy, watery eyes; their balance becomes unsteady and they may have a difficult time standing or walking. Speech also becomes difficult, as they begin to slur words. A very noticeable chemical odor is generally present. You may even notice residue of a substance on a person's nose, mouth, or hands *(photo 10.10)*. Now, look at your child and ask yourself, has their physical appearance and motor skills changed. The chemical odors along with any noted changes can be your initial indicators of inhalant abuse.

The following is a list of signs and symptoms associated with inhalant use: volatile solvents and aerosols elevate pulse, blood pressure and temperature; anesthetic gases (nitrous oxide) usually lower pulse and blood pressure.

The following list is observable with any type of inhalant abused: residue of substance (color of paint) on a person; chemical odor; disorientation; dizziness; distorted perception of time and distance; slow, thick, slurred speech; nausea; confusion; flushed face; non-communicative; intense headache; lack of muscle control, including bladder and digestive track; watery eyes; nosebleeds; loss of sense of taste or smell. Continued use can cause damage to the brain, central nervous system, liver, kidneys, and other organs. Deaths can also occur from heart failure, usually from cardiac arrest and from asphyxiation.

Street Terminology		
Volatile Solvents and Aerosols	**Anesthetic Gasses**	**Nitrates**
Gold	Nos	Rush
Silver	Noz	Climax
Locker Room	Laughing Gas	Aroma of Men
Pam	Moon Gas	Amys
Paint	Going to the Doctor	Amyls
Kick	N2	Thrust
Bagging	Shoot the Breeze	Rock Hard
Huffing	Gas	Liquid Gold
Wite-Out	Whippets	Ram
Oz	Buzz Bomb	Kix
Glue		TNT
Gluey		Hardware
Super gold		Snappers
Gladders		Poppers
Glading		Quicksilver
Huffing		Locker Room
Toncho		
Pearls		

CHAPTER 11

Marijuana

Marijuana, or cannabis, is often referred to as the "gateway drug," because it can lead to experimenting with other controlled substances. There has been a steady debate over the years regarding the legalization of marijuana. The advocates cite studies where marijuana helps cancer patients, increases appetite for AIDS patients, reduces intraocular pressure for glaucoma patients, and assists with pain control for various other diseases.

Marinol was developed as a synthetic form of marijuana and will give many of the same pain controlling effects without having the psychedelic experiences as marijuana. I will not debate the legalization of marijuana in this book, but will provide information regarding the physical signs of the ingestion relating to marijuana use.

There are basically four forms of marijuana; the marijuana plant (photo 11.1), hashish, hashish oil, and Marinol. The marijuana plant is cultivated for the buds and flowers of the plant. Growing marijuana is an art in itself, as a grower needs to be able to recognize the male and female plants of the species. The female plants remain separated from the males, so they are unable to germinate. This will produce higher levels of delta-9 tetrahydrocannabinol otherwise known as THC. The greater the level of THC, the longer and more intense the "high" or effects will be. Back in the 1970s the average marijuana cigarette contained approximately 1– 2 percent THC. Now with sophisticated growing systems the THC content can be as high as 40 percent or more. The marijuana grown today is not the same marijuana of 30 years ago.

There are two distinct odors of marijuana. The first odor is raw marijuana, in which the buds, flowers, or leaves are dried *(photo 11.2)* and then generally packaged in plastic baggies. The second odor is that of burnt marijuana, which is also very distinct. What can you do to recognize the odor of marijuana if you have never smelled it before? First of all, if someone describes the odor to you, there is no correct explanation other than "it smells like marijuana." Become involved in your community, as many police departments have citizens' academies where individuals experience some of the duties of a law enforcement officer. During the citizens' academy, instructors may even burn marijuana for students to recognize its odor. There is also incense sold at head shops that has the odor of marijuana when burned.

We have to use all of our senses, especially that of smell, and question strange odors that we detect on our children or in their surroundings. The odor of marijuana permeates clothing and material, then lingers for long periods of time. Simply smell discarded shirts and jackets for the odor of marijuana.

There are basically two ways to ingest marijuana, orally and smoking. The most common is smoking, where the dried buds of the plant are smoked through a variety of paraphernalia *(photo 11.3a, 11.3b, 11.4a, 11.4b, 11.5)*, which vary and are only limited to the imagination and abilities of the manufacturer. They can be as elaborate as a hookah pipe where several individuals can smoke from the same pipe at one time, or can be as simple as creating one from tinfoil. Blunts and marijuana cigarettes are probably two of the most common methods to smoke marijuana. Blunts are cigars in which a large majority of the tobacco material has been removed and replaced with marijuana, which can then be smoked with the appearance of smoking a cigar. Marijuana cigarettes are commonly referred to as "roaches" and are made by using rolling papers in which marijuana is placed and then smoked. Common types of rolling papers include "Top, Zig-Zag and numerous others available at convenience stores. Users do not want to waste any of the drug, so medical hemostats *(photo 11.6)* or tweezers are used to hold the very tip of the marijuana cigarette, which allows them to smoke it to completion.

Oral ingestion consists of eating or sucking on the buds *(photo 11.7);* however, this is not very common. The baking of marijuana in brownies or chocolates for oral ingestion is more common and disguises the substance so it can be used anytime in front of anyone, as it appears the person is eating a brownie *(photo 11.8).*

When smoking marijuana, the effects begin very rapidly, usually within eight to nine seconds; however, the peak effects take place in about ten to thirty minutes. The user will continue to feel high for usually two to three hours even though the physical signs and impairment can last for much longer. Studies have shown that the impairment from smoking marijuana can last for up to twenty-four hours.

So, what about Hemp? Hemp is grown in several countries for use as rope, food products, body lotions and numerous other products. Hemp contains trace amounts of THC, usually 0.2–0.3 percent, where marijuana plants can attain THC levels as high as 40 percent or greater. At the present time, the United States does not allow the cultivation of industrial hemp, which is another issue I will not debate in this book. However, stickers or writings which depict the legalization of hemp can also be indicators of marijuana use. Many individuals believe marijuana and hemp are the same plant, which is false. Numerous products are available on the market today which contains hemp such as paper products, clothing, body care essentials and even food items. Yet, if you ingest these products, you will not get high.

Hashish

Hashish, which is a refined resin of the marijuana plant, is usually imported from Pakistan, Afghanistan, Lebanon and Morocco *(photo 11.9)*. Hash is not very common in the United States but is very popular in Canada. The popularity of marijuana and its higher concentrations of THC make hash less accepted in the U.S. This is probably because of low concentrations of THC contained within the hash, usually around 5 percent. The buds and flowers of the plant are removed and are generally easy to sell because of the higher THC content. The leaves and stems of the plant are then ground down by a variety of different methods to produce hash. The outcome can vary from the manufacturing process; color can range from tan to green to black, and the texture can be very hard, or soft and pliable. Hash is then smoked in a variety of pipes or added to marijuana cigarettes to increase the THC content.

Hash Oil

Hashish oil is a liquid form of marijuana and is also a refined resin of the plant. It is generally made by soaking marijuana in a container of solvent like acetone. After several hours the plant material is removed from the solvent leaving hash oil that contains about 15 percent THC. Users will take marijuana cigarettes and dip them into hash oil to obtain a higher level of THC. Tobacco cigarettes, cigars, and numerous other drugs are also dipped into hash oil for the THC. The color of hash oil varies depending upon the manufacturing process, but is generally black, green, or light red to a dark red color. Both hash and hash oil will still have the odor of marijuana. It doesn't matter the type of marijuana ingested, the physical signs and symptoms will continue to be consistent.

Red Flags for Parents

There are several different signs you can observe to detect marijuana use. One of the first notable signs of use is simply the odor of marijuana. Raw and burnt marijuana was discussed earlier. A raw odor tells you that marijuana is probably hidden somewhere. A burnt marijuana odor tells you it was recently smoked. Again, we have to use all of our senses, especially that of smell.

Look at and smell your kid's clothes. Look for signs of green vegetable material or the odor of burnt marijuana. The clothes themselves can indicate use by simply understanding the drug culture. Look for the emblem of the marijuana plant on hats, T-shirts, key chains, watches, necklaces, and anything else *(photo 11.10, 11.11a, 11.11b)*. One of the most popular slang phrases is "420," which has several meanings throughout the country, such as the universal time to smoke THC, or April 20, which would be the time to plant your THC seeds. Advocates believe eventually marijuana plants will be growing everywhere and it will have to be legalized. Other terms like "fillabong" rather than Billabong, again refer to THC use. So many items refer to or promote drug use right in front of us that we need to educate ourselves and see the obvious.

When you search rooms, the first place to look is in the trash can for stems or seeds. These portions of the marijuana plant contain very little THC and are generally thrown away. Again, searching is important and be sure to open objects that look like brand name products as they can actually be stash cans *(photo 11.12a, 11.12b)*. Numerous items are false containers made to hide drugs. As you can see, things may not always be what they initially appear to be from soda cans to candles to drinking bottles to books. All were made to conceal items, usually drugs. Film canisters are also used to conceal marijuana *(photo 11.13)*. Black lights are commonly used to enhance mood when ingesting marijuana or hallucinogens.

In a vehicle, the same principle applies. The first place to look is the ashtray for stems, seeds, cigar material, and roaches (THC cigarettes) *(photo 11.15, 11.15, 11.16)*. Look on seats and floorboards for vegetable material—THC seeds, broken cigar material to indicate someone rolling blunts, or THC cigars. Press your nose up to the indoor ceiling and smell the headliner of the vehicle, because the marijuana smoke rises and saturates into the fabric. This is indicative of someone smoking marijuana in the vehicle. Hemostats and tweezers with burn marks are also indicative of marijuana ingestion. If you find butane lighters, smell the striker plates, as continued use causes the odor of marijuana to permeate onto the metal. Don't forget that eye drops or lip balms are commonly used with the ingestion of marijuana *(photo 11.17)*.

Take note of bumper stickers on your child's and their friends' vehicles; many display stickers that are pro drug *(photo 11.19, 11.18, 11.19a, 11.19b, 11.20, 11.21)*. Examples would be "420," an interstate symbol with the highway listed as 420; some that say "248 joints in the human body and none in my pocket," "419 got a minute" (which equals 420), and marijuana leaf symbols. Other stickers displayed may be of music bands which are known to sing songs about drug use, such as Grateful Dead stickers, that include skulls, dancing teddy bears, and skeleton people. Other performers that make drug references include Bob Marley, Jimmy Hendrix, Phish and the list continues on. I'm not saying everyone who listens to these bands are drug users; however, a portion of the population who listen to them also use controlled substances. Also take note of law enforcement and religious stickers, as these are displayed on vehicles to camouflage drug use and mislead the police during traffic stops. I cannot tell you how many traffic stops I have had where I have arrested individuals for drug use or possession and have noted D.A.R.E., support of law enforcement, or religious stickers on the windows or bumpers of the car. Numerous air fresheners including the hanging type, spray bottles, vent air fresheners and even stick-ups are used to cover or mask the odor of illicit drugs *(photo 11.22, 11.23, 11.24, 11.25)*.

Drugs are often transported in vehicles, with the substance usually being picked up in a large city and taken back to smaller or rural areas for continued distribution. Kids will often use their parents' or friends' cars to transport the drugs, as many are aware that if they own the vehicle and drugs are found, the police can confiscate the vehicle. If the vehicle is owned by another individual and drugs are located, the ability of the police to seize the vehicle is much more difficult.

Physical Signs Associated with Marijuana

There are numerous health concerns regarding the ingestion of marijuana. The tar or resin that develops in a person's lungs is about ten times worse than that of smoking cigarettes. Many users develop chronic bronchitis and emphysema over time.

Marijuana is a vasodilator, which means it will cause the white portions of the eyes to become noticeably bloodshot. Therefore, users will carry Visine or Murine to get the red out of the eyes. Marijuana can also cause the pupils of the eyes to become dilated. A person's lips can become dried and cracked from smoking marijuana so users will also carry lip balm or ChapStick to moisten their lips. Knowing this, watch for the continued licking of the inside of the mouth or the repeated drinking of beverages, as the smoking of marijuana causes a dry mouth.

The following is a list of signs and symptoms associated with marijuana use: blood pressure and pulse rate are elevated; however, the body temperature is generally normal. The white portion of the eyes becomes markedly red; the odor of burnt or raw marijuana can be noted on a person's breath or clothing; teeth discoloration *(photo 11.26)*; body tremors; relaxed inhibition; increased appetite; impaired perception of time and distance; disorientation; possible paranoia; short-time memory loss; inability to concentrate; inappropriate laughter; possible anxiety and panic attacks. Continued use can lead to lung cancer, emphysema, bronchitis, and other medical problems.

Common Street Terms

Marijuana		Hash
Buddha	Joint	Patties
Chronic	Yesca	Soles
Reefer	Rambo	Candy Bars
Mary Jane	Indica	Morocco Black
MJ	BC	Blonde
Sweet Mary Jane	Northern Lights	Leb
Pot	Doobie	Black Afghani
Sinsemilla	Honey Blunts	Shish
Roach	Blunts	Kif
Ganja	Mota	Nup
Grass	Astro Turf	Charas
Weed	Ditch Weed	
Dope	Texas Tea	
Bud	Space Cake	
Herb	Wacky Weed	
Bowl	Acapulco Gold	
Maui Waui	Panama Gold	
Alice B.Toklas		

CHAPTER 12

Combining Drugs

Now that we have talked about all the different types of drugs and their predictable effects, it is time to think outside of the box and expand on this information. Not all drug users consume only one type of drug. So what happens to their bodies when they consume more than one category of drugs? There are basically four different effects that can occur. The first is the "Null Effect." This means that when two drugs are consumed and neither has a specific effect, then that effect will not be observed. I know this may sound confusing, but let us think of a drug that does not dilate the pupils. You should have come up with depressants, inhalants or disassociate anesthetics. None of these categories will dilate the pupils. Therefore, combining any of these drugs will not dilate the pupils (this does not include the exceptions we talked about earlier).

The second effect is the "Additive Effect." This means that one drug causes a specific effect and another drug taken in combination also causes the same effect. Now think of a drug that dilates the pupils. You should have come up with a hallucinogen, stimulant or marijuana. Each one of these drugs will dilate the pupils, so when taken in combination, they will cause the pupils to become extremely dilated.

The third effect is the "Overlapping Effect." This means that two drugs are taken in combination, with one drug causing an effect and the other drug does not cause the same effect. Now think of a drug that dilates the pupils and one that does not cause pupil dilation. You should have come up with a stimulant, hallucinogen or marijuana as the drug that dilates the pupils and a depressant, inhalant or disassociate anesthetic for drugs that do not affect pupil size. So what will happen when a drug that dilates the pupils is taken in conjunction with a drug that does not affect the pupil size? The pupils will be dilated because one drug causes the pupil dilation and the other does not affect the pupil size.

The last effect is the "Antagonistic Effect." This is when one drug is taken and it causes an effect and a second drug is ingested and causes the opposite effect. Now think of a drug that dilates the pupils, then think of a drug that constricts the pupils. The drugs that dilate the pupils would be a stimulant, hallucinogen or marijuana. The drug which constricts the pupils would be narcotic analgesics. When combining a drug that dilates the pupils with one that constricts the pupils, it is unknown what the pupil size would be. The pupil size could be dilated, normal, or constricted— it just depends on how much of the drugs were ingested and how much time had passed before you observed the person's eyes. Just remember, the eyes work as a team and if one eye is affected by drugs, the other will also be affected. If one pupil is extremely large and the other is extremely small, it is not a combination of drugs but a medical condition.

We have only discussed and given examples of how combining drugs affects pupil sizes. Now let us look at how other systems of the body could be affected by combining drugs. What would happen if a person were to take a narcotic in combination with a depressant? This is a very common combination. Remember, both drug categories will lower pulse rates, blood pressures, and act like sedatives; respiration will decrease and a person could slip into a coma.

It doesn't matter the types of drugs ingested, as the combining of drugs can cause a variety of effects. If a person were to ingest cocaine and ketamine, one is a stimulant and the other is a dissociative anesthetic, yet both will elevate pulse, blood pressure, and body temperature, increasing the risk of cardiac arrest. A person using drugs runs the risk of severe injury or death each time they ingest a substance. Taking drugs is like playing Russian roulette, and by combining drugs, it increases the risk of death even further.

Don't think that it is just the combining of illegal drugs that can be deadly. Consider a person who consumes legal substances from within the same category. For example, a person drinks Red Bull in combination with ingesting pseudophed, which are both stimulants. This will cause an additive effect and a person will appear hyperactive, be unable to sit still, and their pulse, blood pressure, and body temperature will all elevate to an unknown level. Again, it increases the risk of cardiac arrest, and yet, these are both legal substances.

It can be very difficult to figure out what types of drugs a person is under the influence of, especially if the person is combining various substances to obtain a variety of effects. If you feel more than one drug category is being ingested, look back at each chapter and read over the physical signs and symptoms, as this can be a guide. It is just like consuming alcohol; we can predict general behaviors, but some individuals react differently. Because this can be a very difficult challenge, you may want to seek out professional help.

Street Terms for Commonly Combined Drugs	
Speedball:	Cocaine and Heroin
Trolling:	MDMA and LSD
Peace Weed:	Marijuana and PCP
Fireball:	Cocaine and PCP
Spacebase:	Cocaine and PCP
Sheetrock:	Crack and LSD
Harvey Wallbanger:	LSD and STP
Crack Weed:	Marijuana and Crack
Candy Flipping:	MDMA and LSD
Clickems or Clickers:	Marijuana and Formaldehyde
Poorman's Speedball:	Pseudophed and Codeine
Cheese:	Heroin, Acetaminophen and Diphenhydramine

Mental Disorder or Drug Usage?

One of the most difficult problems is trying to determine if drugs are affecting your child's behavior, if it is a mental disorder or disease, or if the child is simply entering puberty and is just plain moody. Remember, we need to look at the totality of the circumstances. Some questions to ask yourself are has my child's behavior changed in any way, and if yes, how. Does the behavior fit in with any of the categories of drugs we have discussed? Has there been a change in friends or peers? Did you also observe physical changes or changes in hygiene? Have you also observed elevated body temperatures, pulse, or blood pressure? Or have you found any of the drug paraphernalia previously described?

Red Flags for Parents

Now that we understand the physiology of drugs in relation to the human body and the paraphernalia associated with each category, the question remains as to why individuals choose to use drugs. Some kids cave in to peer pressure, while others are trying to fit into a group. It could also be that the child was mistreated at home or school and began using drugs as a way to escape. Other kids are loners and have difficultly meeting friends or have a difficult time fitting in. Drug users form a group and it becomes a place to fit in. Kids in metropolitan areas are also brought into the drug business by being paid cash to be lookouts for police or undercover drug agents. Once being paid, many of the same kids begin to experiment with drugs.

Even the children of the rich and powerful are not exempt from becoming involved in drug use. It could be from the pressure to succeed, or excel and be better than others, or it could simply be that they are bored.

Kids who become addicted to various substances begin to experience a variety of problems such as health-related issues, poor hygiene, and mental changes. They may become secretive about what they are doing and withdraw from family and friends. Their attitudes may become disrespectful and they may experience mood swings. Because drugs affect various chemicals in the brain, their mental abilities may deteriorate. Their involvement in school or extracurricular activities may decline by missing or dropping classes, along with declining grades. This difficulty in school can affect their ability to build positive relationships and attend social events. Friendships may end with different relationships developing. As drug use takes over, material items become less important and may result in a selling of their possessions to pay for the continued supply of drugs. As their life is in a downward spiral, the loss of a job or social status becomes less and less important. If these behaviors continue, eventually they will become involved in the criminal justice system. At that point, it becomes increasingly difficult to return to a normal life. The majority of kids who are questioned about drug use will deny it. Building a rapport with your kids and talking about the harm of drugs with them can help in steering them clear of the drug world.

By far the worst reason kids use drugs is because it is in the family and is being used by their parents or siblings. Let me give you an example; while teaching in Arizona I interviewed a twenty-one-year-old female who had no teeth left, was crying, and actually wanted to stay in jail because she did not want to go back home where her brothers and mother use methamphetamine. She knew if she was released, she would return to the same environment and be exposed to the continued pressure of methamphetamine use. When I asked why she started using drugs in the first place, she informed me that when she was in second grade she came home from school and her mother handed her a glass pipe containing methamphetamine and told her to try it. She stated that it then became a nightly thing. I'm sure you can't imagine exposing your seven-year-old child to drugs, let alone giving them the drugs. Many kids never have a chance because of the environment they are raised in.

CHAPTER 13

How To Search

Room Searches

Some of the topics being discussed in this chapter are controversial and, of course, each parent has the right to make their own choices based on their beliefs. I am going to provide the information and whether you choose to use it, is up to you as an individual.

Many parents search their children's rooms and vehicles, and many other parents feel it is a violation of privacy. As far as the law is concerned, depending on the area of the country in which you live, as long as the child is not paying rent, parents have the right to search. However, if you don't know what you are searching for your search may be useless.

You may have located drug paraphernalia in your child's possessions or their vehicles, either by accident or on purpose. When searching I highly suggest using rubber or latex gloves, as some drugs are absorbed through the skin. While searching the bedroom, one of the priority places to check is the wastebasket. Look for those items that do not fit with the rest of the trash, and if something is suspicious, question it. The stems of the marijuana plant are generally useless and are thrown away, sometimes wrapped in paper to conceal them.

Locating paraphernalia is a big clue to drug use. Make use of the photos and Red Flags for Parents referenced throughout this book. This generation is different from other generations. It's all part of the excitement for them to openly flaunt the clues of their drug use in front of authority.

If searching, don't overlook the obvious. Take note of the posters hanging in your child's room or T-shirts they may be wearing. If they contain marijuana leaf symbols, mushrooms, pixie fairies, toads and frogs, Sesame Street characters with dilated pupils and red eyes, Grateful Dead symbols, dancing teddy bears, skulls with the peace symbol marked in the head, or Gumby, they may relate to drug use. However, you have to look at the totality of your child's behaviors, physical changes, and changes in your child's friends. Just noticing one thing by itself may mean nothing. To determine if drug use is present you need to put all the pieces of the puzzle together.

When searching a room, try to remember back to a time when you were attempting to hide something. Search anywhere and everywhere. Look up, down, and all around. Leave no stone unturned. Look in books and folders. Read them. Kids often times mark up the surfaces of these items. Pay attention to the scribbling on folders. Terms like "Jonesen, Blue Mondays, Terrible Tuesdays, 420, going robo, and special K" all relate to drug use.

Look for empty soda cans with burn marks on the side and holes punched on the opposite side. These are easy-to-make marijuana pipes. Also look for tin foil that has been shaped into a cylindrical object, which is used to smoke marijuana. Along with this look for brass screens, like the ones used in plumbing for sink faucets, as they go inside of the pipes to hold the marijuana.

The terminology of drug use also varies across the United States. There are some drug terms that are popular in one area and not in another. Even the drug of choice can be different from one side of a state to the other. Do not feel guilty for searching your child's room. They are your responsibility and their life can depend on you.

Computer Searches

The internet is known as the "information super highway," which is a great resource for basically any topic; however, it also contains information not suitable for young people. There are chat rooms, which may contain sexual predators; sexual websites, and drug-related websites.

There are several ways of protecting your child from dangerous information on the internet. Software is available that can limit access to the internet and the specific times when a person can log on. Child safety programs are offered from many internet service providers, and software is also available in retail stores. Monitoring tools can also keep track of websites that were visited or give warning when an inappropriate site was accessed. Simply turning on your computer and clicking on the Internet Explorer opens up a tool bar; one of the icons is "history." Click on "history" and you can see what sites your child has recently visited. To change the history setting, double click on tools; a drop-down box appears and then left click on internet options; another tool box opens allowing you to change how long the history saves websites that were visited. Set the "clear history" for twenty days. This will give you ample time to check on websites visited. If you set the history for twenty days and it changes to one, then you know your child is probably visiting inappropriate sites.

The following is a list of websites; some contain educational information, yet others actually promote drug use and even give recipes on how to make certain drugs. Some drugs can also be ordered over the internet from various retail-type stores. The drugs are not cocaine, marijuana, or other illegal substances; however, prescription drugs, homeopathic, and even analogs of drugs can be obtained from various locations on the internet. There are even testimonials by young adults who have experimented with drugs and provide their experiences to readers. They tell what their favorite drugs and combinations of drugs are. Kids who read these testimonials are led to believe the experience will be safe.

Government-related Sites:

U.S. Drug Enforcement
Administration . . . . www.dea.gov

White House Drug Policy . . . www.whitehousedrugpolicy.gov

Painfully Obvious . . . . www.painfullyobvious.com

National Institute on
Drug Abuse . . . . www.drugabuse.gov

Parents The Anti-Drug . . . . . . www.theantidrug.com

Club Drugs . . . . www.clubdrugs.org

Steroid Abuse . . . . www.steroidabuse.org

Street Drugs . . . . www.streetdrugs.org

Join Together . . . . www.jointogether.org

Medical Sites

Web MD . . . . www.webmd.com

RX List . . . . www.rxlist.com

Drug Infonet . . . . www.druginfonet.com

Drug Information Online . . . www.drugs.com

All Purpose Sites

The Vaults of Erowid . . . . www.erowid.org

Graffiti Online Store . . . . www.wellcoolstuff.com

Bouncing Bear Botanicals . . . www.bouncingbearbotanicals.com

Drug Specific Sites
Salvia Divinorum
    Research Site . . . . www.sagewisdom.org
UK Salvia Website. . . . . www.salvia.co.uk
DextroVerse . . . . www.dextroverse.org

Paraphernalia / Clothing Sites
seedleSs Clothing . . . . www.seedlessclothing.com
420 Clothing. www.420pot.com
Headshop . . . . www.headshop.com
Stash Cans . . . . www.stashcans.com

Activist Site
Dance Safe . . . . www.dancesafe.org

Rave and Ecstasy Sites
Candy Kids. . . . . www.candykids.net
MN Vibe. . . . . www.mnvibe.com
Audio Tribe. . . . . www.audiotribe.net

As you can see there is a wide variety of websites with information on drugs, much of which is educational. There are numerous sites which contain pro-drug use. Remember, this can affect your child's life, so do not be afraid to snoop!

Vehicle Searches
When searching a vehicle, whether it is your child's vehicle or a vehicle of your own that your child uses, the first place to start is by walking around the exterior of the vehicle and take note of any

bumper stickers that you find suspicious. Sometimes this is difficult, as the reverse of what you think would be drug use related is
displayed. I have conducted thousands of traffic stops, and during
the course of some of the stops, I have noted religious, D.A.R.E.
and even law enforcement support stickers. These types of stickers
were placed on the vehicle to confuse law enforcement into thinking this person would not be involved in criminal activity when, in
fact, they were involved in criminal activity. Once again, we need
to look at numerous factors, and as I have said throughout this
book, one or two things by themselves may mean nothing. We are
going to look at the totality of the circumstances. A good source
in trying to find out the meanings of the bumper stickers is to look
them up on the internet. And you can always ask your child, but
don't necessarily expect the truth.

The next place to begin searching is the ashtrays throughout
the vehicle. When observing the ashtrays, look for any green stems,
green leaves, or seeds. All are indicative of marijuana use. Also look
for broken up pieces of cigar material, as cigars are cut open with
a razor blade and some of the tobacco is removed and replaced
with marijuana. The cigar is then given the term, "blunt," and
smoked for both the tobacco and marijuana. Generally, the cigars
are smoked down to a one-fourth to one-half inch length; much
more than what a normal cigar is smoked. This is because a person
using drugs wants to get the most out of their money and does not
want to waste drugs they paid for.

Now look at the seats and the floorboards for any of those same
items, as marijuana smokers often times do not clean up the material and, therefore, leave much evidence behind. An excellent way
to determine if individuals have been smoking marijuana in a
vehicle is to smell the headliner, as the smoke permeates into the
cloth and remains for quite a long time.

Kids are smart and will try and thwart your efforts, so look for numerous air fresheners—either spray or pump bottles of air freshener, the hanging type, the can type, the type that go into the vents, the kind that plug into cigarette lighters, or even stick-up air fresheners. If you find dryer sheets or stick-ups placed in the trunk of the vehicle, I would be concerned that larger amounts of drugs are being transported in the cargo area. Air deodorizers are simply used to mask, or attempt to cover up, the odor of marijuana or other drugs. The record number of air fresheners I located in a vehicle was twenty-nine, which was definitely a clue to drug use.

Additional items to look for are ChapStick or lip balm along with Visine eye drops, as both can be used to try and cover up some of the physical signs marijuana induces. As we discussed earlier, marijuana dilates or causes the blood vessels in the eyes to become red; therefore, users often place Visine drops in the eyes to "get the red out." Lip balms are used because smoking marijuana causes the mouth and lips to become dry and possibly cracked.

Continue to search and look for things that are out of the ordinary, such as pieces of a Chore Boy Scrubber in the carpet of the floorboards, on seats, or in the ashtrays. If it is nighttime, simply shine a flashlight onto the carpet and see if a copper color shimmers in the light. The Chore Boy is placed inside of crack pipes to hold the crack rocks in place while smoking. Crack pipes can be glass, copper, metal, just about anything a user can think of.

If cocaine is suspected, look for a white powder residue on the floorboards or in plastic baggies. The baggies may have the corner torn off; this is because the cocaine was placed in the corner of the bag, and then the bag was twisted and pulled apart. The baggie is then tied off for transport or storage. If the baggies were pulled apart, you will find small plastic knots lying around inside the vehicle. Drinking straws are cut down to about three to four inches and are used to snort cocaine, which means you also need to be cognizant of razor blades and a mirror. Cocaine is placed on a mirror and the razor blade is used to make small lines of the powder for snorting. Generally, you won't find Visine, since cocaine is a vasoconstrictor and shrinks the blood vessels of the eyes causing extremely white eyes. However, Carmex or lip balms are again used to aid with the dry mouth and lips.

These are illegal items you think your child would never use. There are many legal over-the-counter items that are available and many can be just as dangerous. Abuse of Robitussin or Delsym cough syrup or blister packs of Coricidin Cough and Cold HBP are also commonly abused drugs, which the majority of the time goes overlooked, even by law enforcement.

The list is endless regarding paraphernalia associated with drug use. Hopefully, the preceding chapters provided a better understanding of the drug culture, and the photos included provided you with the information needed to identify controlled substances and the associated paraphernalia.

We have been blessed with five senses. We need to use four out of the fives senses when actively searching for drugs, and those are: seeing, hearing, touching, and smelling. Never, never use your sense of taste! Then act on what you have observed, but it is best not to accuse unless you have evidence in hand. Once again, whenever searching use rubber or latex gloves as some drugs are transdermal, which means they can be absorbed into the body through the skin. I understand this sounds strange, as this is your child and you don't expect to find any problems. It is still better to be safe than risk your own health.

If you choose to call law enforcement because of items you have located, be aware that the probability of an arrest is likely. You may choose to seek professional counseling for your child's problem as the initial step before turning to law enforcement. Either route you take, remember, your actions could save your child's life.

CHAPTER 14

Conclusion

Some parents allow their teenagers to throw parties where alcohol or even marijuana is present. Not only are the parents committing a crime in most states, they are condoning and promoting drug use. We, as parents, have a right to know what is expected at a party being given by another parent. We don't expect our children's lives to be put at risk when going to a friend's house.

I hope this book has opened your eyes to the behaviors of our children and has provided useful information to intercede or prevent possible disasters in your family's future. I pray you never have to use this information with regard to your children, as when drugs enter the family, it is usually a difficult road to eliminate the use of substances. Families are torn apart by drug use, which usually entails lies, stealing, deceit, and a host of other disturbing behaviors. Just remember, one thing by itself may mean nothing, it is a combination of behaviors, physical signs, and suspicious items that leads to determining drug use. Stay informed, the drug world is constantly changing and new drugs are being developed every day.

Search, search, and search. If you want to know what is going on in your child's life, don't be afraid to search. It could save their life. The greatest thing you can do to prevent drug use is to talk with your child about the effects of drugs; show them the photographs of the drug users in this book. Look on the internet for more pictures and, if possible, take them on a tour of a local jail. And if you really want to know what drugs are in your communities, talk with local police officers, especially school resource officers who really have a handle on the drugs being abused by kids. Police are a great resource, and many are more than willing to inform parents of what they are finding in the community. Again, I don't want to make you paranoid about your child using drugs, I just want you to be informed and to keep an open mind, but also a suspicious one!

Remember, you have raised your children and know their behaviors, their likes, and dislikes. You just have to remain open to the thought that your child could use drugs. Don't be the parent who says, "My Child Wouldn't Do That," or the other famous line, "Not My Child," because you may only be fooling yourself and hurting your child!

CHAPTER 15

About The Author

I was born in 1966 and raised in a small Midwestern town where I lived my whole life. I am the youngest of four children raised by parents who taught us the value of hard work, the importance of honesty and integrity, and I carry those lessons with me today. I am grateful to my parents for financing my education recognizing it required sacrifices from them. My wife, Deb, was the first person who supported my decision to begin a career in law enforcement. Life in law enforcement is not always easy on a family. I have spent my whole career working night shift, and attending substantial specialized training, which resulted in missing many functions and time away from our family. But somehow, during my 21-year career, we managed to raise four children, three of whom have become successful adults and one who is growing up too fast.

I am not a psychologist nor do I hold a Ph.D. I have been a law enforcement officer since 1987, and the information in this book is written from the various incidents I have observed, been involved in or researched. I started my career at the Manitowoc County Sheriff's Department. I am currently assigned to the patrol division working the night shift. I am a K-9 handler and lost my first partner in August of 2004. During our six and a half years together we made thousands of drug arrests, resulting in the seizure of hundreds of thousands of dollars worth of controlled substances, vehicles, and cash from various cases. In 2005, I was given the opportunity to have a second K-9 partner named Kilo.

I received extensive training through the Drug Evaluation and Classification Program sponsored by the National Highway Traffic Safety Administration certifying me as a Drug Recognition Expert.

In September and October of 1996, I attended training in Minneapolis, Minnesota, and was certified as a Drug Recognition Expert Instructor. Along with other officers, I have represented Wisconsin at several National Conferences in Colorado, Oregon, California, New York, Texas, Maryland, Florida and Arizona, on the physiological effects drugs induce on the body.

I have trained thousands of law enforcement officers across the United States. In 2000, I taught at the National Sheriff's Conference in Columbus, Ohio, and in 2002 and 2003 was the course manager for the Wisconsin Drug Recognition Expert Course. In 2006, I was one of the key instructors who helped bring DRE to the State of West Virginia. I also participate in the Wisconsin oversight committee for the state's Drug Recognition Expert Program, and am currently the Region 2 Coordinator for the Program. I also instruct various drug courses for the Multijurisdictional Counterdrug Task Force for St. Petersburg College, instructing agents from the Drug Enforcement Administration, United States Border Patrol, Chicago and New York PDs, along with officers from throughout the country. I was privileged to have had the opportunity to fly with the United States Border Patrol, Tucson sector, attempting to locate illegal aliens and drug smugglers. I also spent time at the Douglas County Port of Entry with U.S. Customs.

Throughout the course of my career I have attended numerous specialized schools and seminars in the area of narcotics enforcement: drug impaired and intoxicated drivers, drug interdiction, advanced interdiction, commercial motor vehicle interdiction, basic narcotics investigation, DEA pipeline, and numerous other courses. I also hold certifications as an instructor in Standardized Field Sobriety Testing, Drug Recognition Expert, Drug Interdiction, Vehicle Contacts, Cultural Diversity and Ethics, The Complete Traffic Stop, and Drug Impairment Training for Education Professionals.

5.1 Numerous products contain ethanol including flavorings, mouthwash, beer, wine, and distilled spirits.

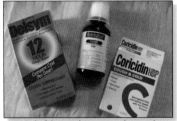

5.2 Each of these products contains dextromethorphan. Delsym is often mixed with orange soda.

5.3 Alprazolam is a common antidepressant being abused.

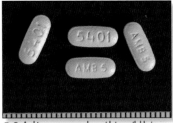

5.3 Ambien, a common sleep aid, is available in different dosages. Pictured here are 5 mg tablets.

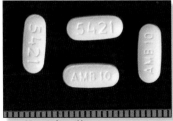

5.5 10 mg Ambien tablets.

5.6 Clonazepam 5/10 mg tablets. Calling Poison Control Center at 1-800-222-1222 could easily identify the pills with a description.

5.7 Color and shape of prescription pills can vary depending on the manufacturer. Pictured are two examples of 2 mg diazepam tablets. .

5.8 Dosing of GHB is dangerous, as a variation of a few grams can be fatal. A capful of GHB can render unsuspecting victims comatose or cause death.

135

5.9 Color of GHB can vary just by adding food coloring. Note the water bottles with what should be a clear liquid contain a bright blue liquid.

5.10 GHB is commonly contained in sports drinks and water bottles.

5.11 If GHB is contained in noncarbonated sports drinks or water, it may foam or become cloudy when shaken.

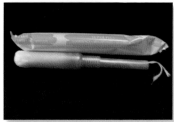

5.12 Tampons are soaked in GHB and inserted rectally.

5.13 There are hundreds of products on the market containing GHB or analogs of GHB.

5.14 Once Removed Nail Polish Remover used to contain butyrolactone which metabolizes into GHB. Yes, kids were drinking it.

5.15 Valerian root is a natural sleep aid that does not contain GHB but will cause heavy sedation.

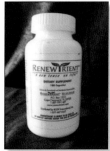

5.16 Renewtrient is advertised as not containing GHB. It does contain GBL, which metabolizes in the body into GHB.

6.1 Energy drinks usually contain large amounts of caffeine and other stimulating substances that can create health problems.

6.2 A variety of energy pills are available. Tobacco-free Ecstasy cigarettes are legal for kids to purchase and contain caffeine. Catnip is also smoked.

6.3 Khat contains cathinone a scheduled I drug and is smuggled into the United States from East Africa, Somalia and the Arabian Peninsula.

6.4 Nine ounces of powdered cocaine has an approximate street value of $25,000 depending on the area of the country.

6.5 Pictured is 1 gram of cocaine with a street value of about $100. One gram yields approximately 20 to 30 one-inch lines for snorting.

6.6 Bindles are glossy papers that contain about 1 gram of cocaine. Cocaine may be placed on a mirror, divided into lines, and snorted.

6.7 Powdered cocaine was placed on the underside of a pet's toy and the shortened straw was then used to snort the cocaine.

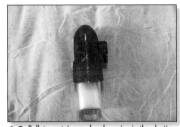

6.8 Bullets contain powdered cocaine in the plastic or glass tube and are tipped over where a valve allows the desired amount of cocaine to be ingested.

6.9 This close up picture of "crack cocaine" depicts the off white to white color of the substance.

6.10 Crack rocks can also be hidden in glass vials.

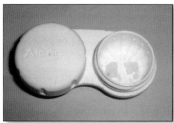

6.11 Pieces of crack cocaine hidden in a contact case—remember, drugs can be very small and hidden in all kinds of places, so search thoroughly.

6.12 The glass crack pipe in the center was concealed in the cigarette pack; small plastic pieces contained crack cocaine; digital scale weighed cocaine.

6.13 Crack pipes can also be elaborate. Note the small plastic baggies containing crack rocks. One uses a zip-lock seal; the others are a bag's knotted corner.

6.14 Crack pipes can be glass or metal; even broken car antennas. Chore Boy is placed inside the pipe to hold the crack rocks in place while they are smoked.

6.15 Pipes are usually cylindrical and may have tape on the ends or in the center. The tape is used to protect lips and fingertips from the intense heat.

6.16 Weapons and unexplained money are often consistent with the sale of drugs. Baking soda is for cutting and plastic baggies are for packaging cocaine.

6.17 Crown Royal bags often conceal drugs. Crack cocaine was placed in the glass flower-holder tubes. Chore Boy held crack rocks in place in the glass tubes.

6.18 Pieces of Chore Boy on the floorboards of a car are indicative of smoking crack.

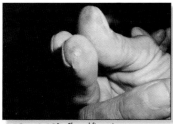

6.19a, 6.19b Charred fingertips are common among users who smoke stimulants, methamphetamine, or other illegal drugs. The glass and metal pipes burn at very high temperatures causing the fingertips to get burned.

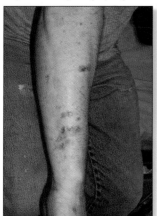

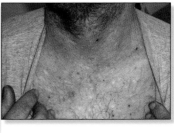

6.20a, 6.20b Coke bugs or snow bugs are street terms referring to users who pick at their skin because of cocaine use.

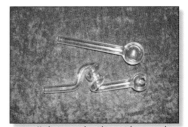

6.21 Meth pipes can be either straight or curved tubes with a bulb on the bottom, or can be hollowed out light bulbs.

139

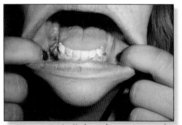
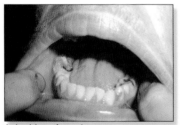

6.22a, 6.22b Meth-mouth—a street term that indicates the breakdown of enamel and the loss of teeth. Note the broken off teeth and infection. Odor is quite pungent.

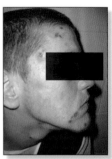
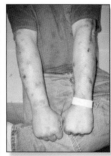

6.23a, 6.23b, 6.23c Meth bugs or crank bugs are street terms associated with users who pick at their skin. Common areas are face, arms, legs, and back of the head.

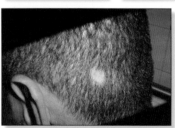

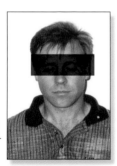

6.24 The temperature was 20° F when contact was made with this subject. Note perspiration-soaked clothing. Stimulants elevate body temperatures.

7.1 Psilocybin mushrooms are known for their hallucinogenic effects. The stems of the plant, along with the buttons, are depicted.

7.2 Seeds of the Jimsonweed plant are ingested for the hallucinogenic effect.

7.3 Peyote, which contains the hallucinogenic chemical mescaline, has been used in Native American rituals for centuries.

7.4 Nutmeg and morning glory seeds are natural hallucinogens.

7.5 Although one item by itself can mean nothing, a mushroom key chain could hint to possible use of psilocybin mushrooms.

7.6 Tattoos can also contain indicators of drug use like the mushroom depicted on the subjects arm.

7.8a, 7.8b The inside of surgical masks and carpenters masks are smeared with Vicks VapoRub as senses are again heightened from ecstasy use.

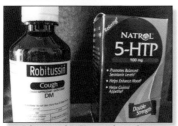

7.7 Robitussin and 5-HTP are used in combination with ecstasy to help balance serotonin levels.

7.9a, 7.9b Rave paraphernalia can be completely legal (glow sticks, spinning lights, fans with lights, brilliant laser light shows, disco balls, or multi-colored rotating globes of light). As individuals stare into the lights, their c senses are overwhelmed.

7.10 Various candies and over-the-counter pill bottles—users often mix ecstasy tablets with legal items.

7.11 Ecstasy tablets can vary in size and shape and will depict various symbols such as king's crowns, superman logo, flowers, and many others.

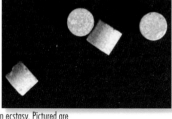

7.12a, 7.12b Many pills sold as ecstasy do not even contain ecstasy. Pictured are LSD tablets.

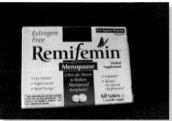

7.13 The purchaser of these tablets attempted to conceal them in a Tylenol bottle.

7.14 These menopausal pills have a butterfly imprint and are sold to unsuspecting teens as ecstasy.

7.15a, 7.15b, 7.15c LSD blotter paper commonly has cartoon characters or other colorful symbols imprinted on them to attract kids. The blotter paper is commonly ingested by placing it on the tongue.

7.16 Rave items may include fans, colored lights, glow sticks, pacifiers, carpenter or surgical masks, Vicks VapoRub and Vicks nasal inhaler, gardening or plush gloves, Pez, Altoids, candy necklaces, and anything that could conceal or contain pills.

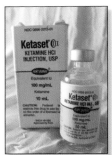

8.1 Bottles of ketamine that may sell on the street for $200 are commonly stolen from veterinarian clinics.

9.1a, 9.1b, 9.1c The color and consistency of heroin vary depending upon the manufacturing process. Depicted is white, black tar, and brown.

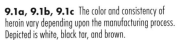

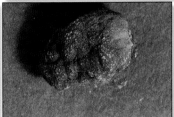

143

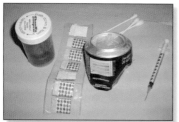

9.2 Drug bags often show a dealer's design. Pill bottle holds water, cotton from Q-tip is filter, torn soda can is cooking container.

9.3 An amount of heroin is placed on the spoon, and a small amount of water is then placed over the heroin. The heroin is "cooked up" using a lighter.

9.4 A cotton ball or cigarette filter tip is placed in the spoon over the cooked heroin. Heroin is drawn up into the needle through the cotton ball filter.

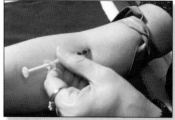

9.5 The heroin is then ready to be injected into a vein, artery, or muscle tissue.

9.6 No spoon was available, so the bottom of a soda can was used to cook up heroin.

9.7 The pea-sized cotton balls contain trace amounts of injectable drug. Users may add water, cook, and squeeze them, or the balls may be sucked on.

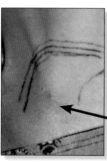

9.8 The female injected into the carotid artery in the neck, which is extremely danger-ous. Notice the bruising.

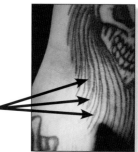

9.9 Tattoos are a great place to hide injection marks. The wider hairs are areas where the individual injected into the tattoo causing the ink to bleed out.

9.10 Pictured here are 80 mg tablets of oxycodone.

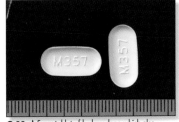

9.11 A 5 mg tablet of hydrocodone which also contains 500 mg of acetaminophen.

9.13, 9.14 Fentanyl and morphine patches absorb into the body and are easily hid under clothing. Actiq suckers contain fentanyl.

9.12 Pictured are a 15 mg and 10 mg Morphine Sulfate tablet.

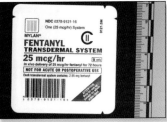

9.15 Codeine is contained in many prescription cough syrups. This one contains codeine and guaifenesin, which is a cough expectorant and decongestant.

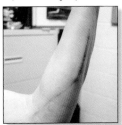

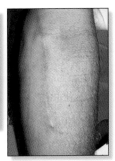

9.16a, 9.16b, 9.16c Numerous track marks can be observed on the hands and elbows of these individuals.

9.17 The outline of what appears to be a large bandage on this user's ribs is actually from fentanyl patches left on the skin.

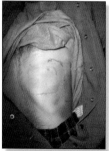

9.18a, 9.18b Constricted pupils and droopy eyelids are two of the most obvious signs of narcotics use.

9.19 A basic injection kit contains: tourniquet (belt or rubber band), a hypodermic needle, spoons, bottle caps or soda can bottom, heroin in a small balloon or tin foil, a heat source, cotton balls or filtered cigarette tip, and some water.

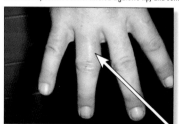

9.20 A missed try at injecting heroin into a vein in the ring finger vein instead injected into the skin, causing a severe reaction and swelling.

10.1 Paint thinner or chemicals of choice are soaked into a rag for inhalation.

10.2 The rag can be held up to the nose and mouth for inhalation or placed into a bag, so the fumes are more concentrated.

10.3 The bag is then placed over the nose and mouth and the volatile solvent inhaled.

10.4 There are thousands of chemicals being abused for recreational purposes.

10.5 "Crackers" are used to expel the nitrous oxide from the cartridges. Crackers come in a variety of shapes and sizes. They can be plastic, glass, or metal.

10.6a, 10.6b, 10.6c, 10.6d A whippet is a container of nitrous oxide used to make whipped cream at coffee houses. The whippet is placed inside the cracker and a balloon is placed over one end. When screwed together, a pin inside punctures the whippet's seal releasing the nitrous oxide into the balloon. This is the same nitrous oxide used at dentist offices across the country.

10.7 The propellant in Reddi-wip contains nitrous oxide.

10.8a, 10.8b The Reddi-wip can is held upright with a balloon over the tip. Pressing discharges the nitrous oxide into the balloon for inhalation. A user feels the effects immediately and may pass out for a short time as the brain is oxygen-deprived.

147

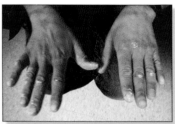

10.10 This person was huffing white paint, although gold and silver paints are preferred. Paint residue remains on lips, face, and hands of users.

11.1 Marijuana leaves generally contain an odd number of leaves; however plants recently discovered in Canada had an even number of leaves.

11.2 Fifteen pounds of marijuana buds recently picked were wrapped in newspaper and allowed to dry.

11.3a, 11.3b Various pipes to smoke marijuana include sockets, toilet paper holder, fake cigarettes, glass pipes, and bongs. Typically, the large cylinder of the bong contains water which both filters and cools the marijuana. Many of these products are legally sold as tobacco smoking devices.

11.4a, 11.4b A lip stick holder is actually a marijuana pipe.

11.5 The Mojo pager is actually a marijuana stash box containing a one-hitter in the shape of a battery.

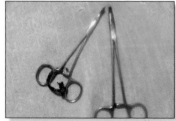

11.6 Hemostats are commonly used to hold marijuana cigarettes. Notice the burn marks on the tips.

148

11.7 Buds of the marijuana plant contain the highest levels of THC.

11.8 Marijuana brownies, known as Alice B. Toklas, are made to conceal marijuana and can then be eaten in front of anyone.

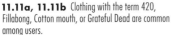

11.9 Hashish is a hardened resin form of marijuana and is not very common in the United States.

11.10 Lighters, air fresheners, key chains, John Deere wrist bands and T-shirts (John Deere tractors cut "grass"), and marijuana scents are also red flags.

11.11a, 11.11b Clothing with the term 420, Fillabong, Cotton mouth, or Grateful Dead are common among users.

11.12a, 11.12b Stash cans ("California Safes") look like common products and are sold to hide valuables, but tops or bottoms of these items unscrew.

11.13 Film canisters are a common method to conceal marijuana.

11.14 Marijuana, when rolled into a cigarette, is referred to as a "joint."

11.15 Marijuana seeds or buds are often forgotten in the ashtray of a vehicle.

11.16 Broken pieces of cigar material on floorboards or ashtrays of vehicles are indicative to smoking blunts. Blunts are hollowed-out cigars filled with marijuana.

11.17 Users often use Visine to reduce the redness in the eyes and may also use also Carmex to relieve chapped lips from smoking.

11.18 Look for magazines like *High Times* and *Heads,* or bumper stickers supporting marijuana use, or hemp necklaces, chains, or earrings depicting marijuana.

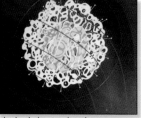

11.19a, 11.19b Logos for Grateful Dead, Phish, or other bands that sing about drug use are placed on vehicles to show support of drug use. Or, users may display pro-law enforcement stickers to try to fool parents or authorities. If you are unsure of a band, look them up on the internet.

11.20 The term "eight ball" is synonymous with the weighing of drugs. This eight ball symbol was displayed on the antenna of a car.

11.21 Drug-related symbols drawn on the headliner of a vehicle.

11.22 Hemp necklaces and numerous air fresheners hanging from the rearview mirror of the car are additional red flags.

11.23 Look for multiple air fresheners in vehicles (especially in the trunk), hemp lip balm, toilet paper rolls with fabric softener inside, or patchouli oil.

11.24 Urine cleansers are used too.

11.25 A Crown Royal bag hanging from the shifter column of this vehicle contained a marijuana pipe.

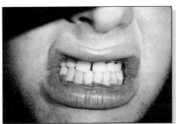

11.26 Discoloration of teeth or greening, as in this case, can be an effect of prolonged marijuana use.

BIBLIOGRAPHY

Amera-Chem, Inc. *Drug Identification Bible.*
Grand Junction: 2003
www.drugidbible.com

Joseph, Donald. *Drugs of Abuse.* Arlington:
Drug Enforcement Administration 2003.
www.dea.gov

Porratta, Trinka. Project GHB.
http://www.projectghb.org

The International Drug Evaluation and Classification Program
Drug Recognition Expert Instructor Manual 2006
www.decp.org

SynergEbooks

Taking Books to New Heights